Communicat | Conflict | Stress

Leadership

Time

Soft Skills
Articles

Anger

EQ

DR.KRISHNA SURESH

Preface

I am much obliged to you for selecting to read, download this book. My solitary motive was to put all my work, study on soft skills in a simpler form which would empower individuals of varying backgrounds becoming more acquainted with ,what soft skills are. Anybody is welcome to reach out to me for any elucidation with respect to these themes on Soft Skills. As a Trainer, I have drafted these short essays for the Students, Corporate, and Bankers for better insightfulness. Anybody can get trained in these skills. Together with this I give the training system I adopt in my training for better consideration. This training would be relevant for everyone who seeks Soft Skills for enhancing their Prospects in their career. Here are the few means which I follow.

Power Point Presentation

This technique is viable when a significant measure of data is required to be imparted in a brief timeframe. Be that as it may, but a viable and an effective presentation considers communication between the trainer and the participants.

Group Discussion

The participants looks at an issue or the subject of eagerness with the objective of a superior comprehension of an issue or ability, achieving the best arrangement or growing new thoughts and headings for the gathering.

Brainstorming in view of the subject.

Brainstorming is a technique employed for critical thinking or creating diverse conceivable answers for an issue. The reason for brainstorming is to concoct the same number of thoughts as conceivable without respect to quality, with the same number of colleagues as conceivable contributing their contemplations. The quantity of thoughts created is more imperative than their common sense and even the most out of control thoughts are acknowledged furthermore, recorded.

Case Studies

Circumstance examination permits participants to think, dissect and talk about circumstances they might experience. Case studies might be founded on genuine cases or speculative circumstances yet ought to raise main problems. The motivation behind a case study is to give learners a circumstance, giving adequate foundation data to break down and register the result of occasions or to give answers for particular issues.

Activity

The most enthralling aspect of training session is the activities. This makes the participants at ease bringing in the best from them. There are array of activities 1) Quiz contest 2) Ice Breaker 3) Posters and painting competitions 4) Games, Puzzles, storytelling, debate 5) Meditation and visual capturing through guided voice over for a minimum 20 minutes.

Thanks &Regards

Dr.Krishna Suresh M.D (A.M) NLP

sureshkmurthi@gmail.com

Authors Biography

1. Why did you choose your career in training?

Training is more a Passion than a Profession to me. I had been in various domains like Exports of Leather Garments, Imports of Raw Material for Steel Industry and Media in the past. Today training and development plays the most important role in shaping the future India. There is a basic skill which the younger generation should be familiar with, mainly Communication. As everyone is aware lack of proper Communication can lead conflict and poor communication will strain the productivity of the organization. Poor communication in business whether written or oral can hinder the competence of any organization. I chose the domain of training due to unforeseen circumstance, having got into it I am really enjoying this stint as a trainer. My sustained interest in Psychology, NLP pivoted me as a behavioural trainer. I bring forth my long real life experience and my training in the US to guide learners on various flavours of soft skills.

2. What are your areas of interest in training?

My strengths hold up with the Training need of the Organization/Institution. Being multitalented is very much essential in making the session lively. Trainers are no Teachers. The teacher teaches the subject and has no time to get feedback from the student, whereas trainer trains and waits for the feedback to be satisfied with his performance. I perform the training like a stage actor well prepared. I always consider me as the best person who can effectively train; this confidence brings out the best in me and from the participants. My other area of strength is Psychological intervention in the midst of training module, say a case study, current affairs or a short story telling, this fetches the best outcome. I do have the qualities, skills, and experience that make me unique. Summing it my area of Interest in Toto is to comfort every participant, iron out any variation in terms of their understanding.

3. What methodologies do you use in your training, to make it lively and entertaining?

My training methodology will be focused on transferring information. It is always looked into and upgraded. I guarantee that I convey the most upcoming training strategies and methods. I do emphatically trust that actively involved members will assimilate and hold learning much more effectively than gazers. Where material is reviewed and applicable to the members' own encounters, comprehension is essentially developed. My training programmes are intended to give the participants a lively and appropriate learning experience. There are various means in which training is prepared to break the dullness, Icebreakers, storytelling, business simulations, role plays, Interactive group exercise and discussion, inbound outbound team building exercise and customized case studies.

4. What change do you bring to a participant who attends your session?

o   I am entirely different in my approach, I deliver training of various dimension, and the delivery to various groups of participants. My training will be breathtaking for the participants; I do make sure the entire participants involve in the training. The training session brings in the awareness into the participants by enhancing their listening skills, tolerance, organisational and time management skills, and effectiveness in appearance, modern world etiquette, and excellent communication skills. I make sure through my training various tools are made available to mitigate acute stress. A feel of change takes place in their attitude. Not a single participant leaves the arena without learning the training need.

5. What was the successful learning intervention that you implemented so far in your training career?

Building up a training intervention program includes assessing the need, designing training module, creating preparing presentations and activities, executing the program and assessing the achievement of the program. Break down the issue I need to solve. Figure out whether the issue can be moderated or disposed of by giving a guideline that empowers the participants to augment new information, get new ability and figure out how to utilise these imaginative strategies for critical thinking. Planning the training program by distinguishing the training need. List what the members understand or recollected after the session is over, follow up on once training is finished. I encountered a training module preparing for PACS (Primary agricultural cooperative Society) Andhra Pradesh.

6. As a trainer, how do you ensure that everyone in your training session develops their skill?

We know, different people have different learning speed and grasping power.There are various scales in which we can gauge the effectiveness of training. The evaluating process is getting to know, was training delivered as scheduled, on time and to the designated group of Participants? Which training strategies worked with which topic and which strategy slackened? Which method did not get well with the subject matter or group of people? What particular issues happened? How powerful was the trainer at connecting with the group of people and transferring data? Taking these parameters into consideration I don't disregard any participant regardless of every possibility of he tend to dissuade others. I discover his interest and approach the session involving him. I have found in my training everyone has a latent talent, and as a trainer all, we need the patience to bring out that.

7.   What is the best compliment you received for your session?

Bank sub staff to Executives, Jailers, Students, has found my training refreshing and triggering attitudinal change in them. As I was in the process of training Bank staff, it was a session with sub staff. There was a question thrown to every participant who has made a significance contribution in your life. Many participants came with various answers. One participant said "Sir, you are my inspiration, I will contribute my best to the Bank from tomorrow "Many expressed their desire attend training frequently.

8.   Which was your very successful and personally satisfying training experience?

There is a long list of this question. Without satisfaction from both the sides, my training session is incomplete. My overseas training assignment with Global MBA students at Singapore, then Training IFMR Students at Sricity, Andhra o their Industrial preparedness week. Training was very interactive on various soft skill subjects. Training more than 500 staffs of Central Bank of India, Chennai, and Kerala.

Training top executives of TNSC Bank, Exclusive training module preparation and delivery to PACS. The most satisfying experience was the stress management workshop for Puzhal inmates.

9. What has been the most difficult training situation that you have had to deal with?

Initially, it was a bit tough getting the Jailers, warders and the staffs of Puzhal prison into the groove. Understandably their day to day interaction with the inmates has made them a bit unyielding. After ice breaker and when the session picked up, they slowly started participating. Then everything got perfectly blended.

10. Which is your favourite book?

"Emotional Intelligence" by Daniel Goleman.This book has all the nuisances on emotions and also how emotions can be managed intelligently. When HR'S was referring to IQ as appointment barometer, psychologist Michael Goleman turned the Management world towards him with his hypothesis on Emotion. He coined the word 'EQ which is emotional quotient.

11. Who is your Role Model?

I mirror TONY ROBBINS; he is very famous American Success Coach. Tony had a background in psychology; Most of Tony work is NLP related. Robbins began his own work as a self-help coach. Today is net worth is amazing.

12. What quote do you live by?

"BE HAPPY; MAKE OTHERS HAPPY, when you feel good for no reason, the environment responds and the tranquility sets in. Wish everyone with a smile and comforting them with soothing expressions can bring about cheerfulness to you and to others.

13. Who inspired you the most?

Nichiren Buddhist Daisaku Ikeda is my Mentor, a Buddhist philosopher, peace builder, educator, writer and poet. He is the third president of the Soka Gakkai and the founding president of the Soka Gakkai International (SGI) which promotes world peace through Buddhist Practice.

14. Share us a challenge that you faced in your life and the way you overcome the same.

This is Krishna Suresh from Chennai, India. I had always been very autonomous in life. I started my career as a businessman after completion of my studies. I was fairly successful in my Endeavour as a Manufacturing Exporter of Leather, Leather Garments.

It was in 90's I was perfectly young, basking on a glorious run of my leather garment export business, even in the wildest of imagination I would have ever thought my life will be taking a deep downside/Nosedive for next decade or so. Yes!! The Road traffic accident was of unusual dimension. I was taken to a nearby hospital. Doctors performed procedures to save my leg as all the blood vessels were ruthlessly damaged. The accident twinge and my financial affliction compounded and there was an array of operation to set correct my busted right leg.

It was a dreadful accident which tossed me out of gears for 5 years in the prime time of my career. I was at the mercy of leading Orthopedicians of Chennai, who tried very hard for union my 5 inches segment loss of femur, nothing went their way. I had to wait 5 long years insulated with Ilizarov apparatus. Since it took too long a time to recover, I was practically immobile with 9 huge rings and 54 pins and wires penetrating my right femur to facilitate the growth of the lost bone, the existing business faded out in my absence and I had to look for other alternative business prospects.

The trauma which I underwent was sheer illogicality, it stretched out for years. My Physical and financial fortune took a vigorous thrashing in this tenure. I was subjected to more than 15 surgeries and 40 times of administration of Anesthesia. I distinguished and encountered Stress of various nature, aspect and levels. Recuperation was delayed. It was five long years with crutches and callipers and step by step tried walking without support.

I was very much inclined to keep my poise. My Intrapersonal and an interpersonal relationship were very much reorganized. Instead of dissonance and diffidence, my attitude and behaviour got perfectly blended and was brimming with only self-belief. All my miseries were mutated with hope.

My Knee and ankle were locked by Doctors to facilitate the union of the fracture. Years rolled I had to close down by the export operation which ran several skilled men jobless. I was fighting against the wall trying to fix my profession.But my enormous coolness in spite of my predicament paved way for new leash of energy.

With my mobility restricted I was perplexed on the mounting weight to my body which was a deterrent for my walking and was beset with diabetic Mellitus. I went for Nature cure Therapy on dieting and weight reduction. It was for sure Social influence made me walk parting my calipers and clutches. Incredible result started flowing, losing more than 15 Kgs weight on dieting and minimum walking.

I was never impatient kept hoping something good would crop up. I happen to discover that I can do exceptionally well in training, teaching and counselling. The pungent lessons learnt in my life were a case-study. This self-awareness propelled me to travel independently to, USA and Canada to explore training possibilities.

 As I had experienced all stressful situations I have the required eligibility to teach on that subject. For this reason, I took soft skills to teach and train, then I added NLP to my study. Through online crash course supplemented up to 15 courses on various soft skill subjects to showcase my learning and training skill.

My articles on soft skills, wellness are published weekly in IT News Paper. Professionally I look for Opportunities to train, coach, motivate people and trigger unlocking the potential in them. I am really elated with my profession as a Soft Skill/behavioural trainer, which has given me immense fulfilment. Being cultured by Nichiren Buddhism I voluntarily look for people who are suffering, offer them with direction and console them with hope. Many find comfort with my curative practice. I continue to serve people with a stamp of Authority now, as a Registered Doctor of Medicine in Alternative Medicine.

15.   In the competitive and technology ridden world, what changes can you bring?

In today's competitive and technology dominated world communication, conflict Management and Mitigating stress stand tall and which needs immediate focus. The Individual and Management need to address these for better outcome. It necessitates apart from technical training Soft skill/Behavioural training is mandatory for all level in an Organization, Institution.

16) As a Doctor and a Trainer how is that you able to satisfy both your profession?

See, I am Doctor of Alternative Medicine specialising in Counselling, Psychotherapy and Naturopathy. These subjects are in line with training. Delivering a training need these specialised skills like counselling, Psychotherapy. You need to listen what the participant delivers, counselling comes into action. In stress management classes most of the tools are psychotherapy related. So for wellness, and weight reduction naturopathy comes handy. As a doctor individuals are attended in training groups is addressed.

Your message /advice to the youth reading this interview?

Stay Calm, Cool, Collected, never try to manipulate. If you are skill deficient kindly add up to your skills at any given opportunity. Be positive and make sure there is no iota of pessimism in your approach. Always believe you can achieve, for that all you need ability and resourcefulness. Stay Confident. You will surely win.

Regards
Dr Krishna Suresh M.D (A.M) NLP
Doctor OF Medicine in Alternative Medicine
NLP Practitioner
Soft Skill Trainer
Food Safety and Standards; Master Trainer.

Contents

Soft Skills for Present and Future

In the present day, soft skills are the most favoured agenda among all people. In a recent tryst with bankers, corporate and students, it determined that a lot of of them are in need of effective communication. Some of them shared an experience that not all the information they have thought of is being communicated clearly. After coming out of the dialogue, various individuals reflect they could have given information that is more pertinent. There are reasons, which are hindering these compelling performers.

They could be broadly categorised,

1) Communication, Listening

2) Effective Speaking

3) Stress related inhibitions.

Solution to this is Soft Skill, it edifies every interaction can be made lively, understanding from the adage, all of us have come to this world alone and will leave alone, but we cannot live alone. We have to necessarily communicate with people known or unknown.

Listening is an art as Dalai Lama states, "You learn when you listen to others, however when you prefer to talk, you are only rehearsing what you already know." The first and foremost lessons to be learnt in communication are to carefully listen to what others articulate during a dialogue.

Secondly, convert all dialogue into a discussion; there should not be any room for argument, an important factor is to welcome any good initiative during a discussion. Neurological studies have observed that speaking raises blood pressure whereas attentive listening can bring it down. The participants in our training hear the instructions, but a majority don't listen. There is a vast difference between hearing and listening. Hearing refers only to the sound and is a physiological function of the ears, whereas listening requires focus and cognition, it needs attention on the delivery, verbal –non-verbal messages, language, and voice modulation.

Scholars have appreciated the importance of communication: as social beings, we cannot exist without communication. The effective communication plays a vivid role; it always carries the emotion and the intent in the message. It is a two-way street, it's about how you convey a message so that it is received and understood by someone in exactly the way you intended while it's also how you listen to gain the full meaning of what's being said and to make the other person feel heard and understood.

Developing effective communication skills begins with simple interactions. Communication skills can be practised every day in settings that range from the social to the professional. Adding new skills take a time to process, but each time when communication skills are used, it opens to new to opportunities and future partnership.

Non-Verbal Communication

By using, gestures, posture, sign, symbol, arms uncrossed, standing with an open stance or sitting on the edge of your seat, and maintaining eye contact with the person you are talking to brings about the efficacy of effective communication through body language.

Employers are looking for people with better emotional skills, such as social awareness, empathy, self-management, the ability to work under stressful conditions, interpersonal skills, proficiency in communication, presenting ideas and negotiation. While the contemporary place of work turns out to be more and more emotionally challenging, professionals need the necessary soft skill tools to help themselves deal with peers, customers and supervisors with professional diplomacy, higher productivity, efficiency, and skilful problem solving.

Stress, A barrier to achieving better skills

During Soft Skill training sessions with the students, I found out that most of the students are stressed on various bases such as arrears, low marks, internships, and placements. The confidence in communicating was very much to be desired.

To communicate effectively, you need to be aware of and in control of your emotions that is managing stress. When stressed, it is more likely to misread other people, send ambiguous messages. Stress results in irritation and anger. Many of us feel stressed during a disagreement with the spouse, kids, boss, friends, or colleague and then later regret it.

Any complex situation warrants only responding not reacting. A reaction is an act of being defensive. In our reactions, our emotions take a vital role. We are uncomfortable with what is being said or done and we instantaneously react, whereas responding is guided less by emotion and more by logic. Reacting is passive in nature, however, a response is more active, and it can change the direction of an interaction.

The training session with Companies, corporate and bankers was very dynamic. The training manual had all the soft skill flavours, energisers, creativity, role-plays, case study, team building, and leadership activities. All the modules were an interfusion of management skills and psychological interventions.

One of the banker participants observed, "The training was refreshing, very informative, de-stressing, me, and my fellow participants believe we need this kind of training every six months. Kindly include this as your suggestion to the management."

Internal cleansing is the order of the day. This needs to be practised without any excuse where a few meditation exercises form the core of the training. This enhances cognition, relieves stress, and makes participants more agile and alert. This has helped few students' to record their triumphs in the ensuing exams and many participants have added new skills to their profiles.

We keep asking questions on Stress, as we have not found an answer to it. We have successfully fought many epidemics, even the recently resurfaced deadly dengue. All these have an exterior cause, but we are now mutely engulfed with the most alarming facet called stress. However, it may not take life instantly but a study has shown it is a silent destructive force.

Companies in these sectors say, IT, BPO, Biotech, and Pharmaceutical industries have found that their staffs/Executives are in need of soft skills to work effectively in cross-functional or project teams, locally and globally. They have to promote their executives faster than before to meet their growth needs. At the same time, they are finding that the candidates do not have the necessary skills to make the transition from a technical or functional expert to a holistic team leader or manager.

Take away: A few years back soft skills weren't always seen as imperative as technical or practical skills to employers, but after profound introspection by HR professionals, it is now noted that soft skills are a must for development, all walks of people need to be familiar with soft skills, in my tenure as a trainer I found students need soft skill for enhancing their careers, Staffs and executives require soft skills for improved performance and to mitigate stress. Bankers are customer oriented, and their added responsibility is recovering bad debts, and redeem Non Performing Assets, to address these it warrants soft skill application. Most of the nationalised/Private bank has started allocating resources for soft skill training. The state and the Central Government can also augment their governance by adequately training their workforce on soft skills. Without soft skill prowess technical training is futile. The future is soft skills.

Soft Skills are progressively turning into the inevitable skills of today's workforce. It's sufficiently not to be profoundly trained only for hard or technical skills, without bridging the interpersonal and relationship abilities that help individuals to communicate and concur cogently.

While your specialized skills may get you to threshold of any gateway, but it is you're communication skills are what open the vast majority of the ways to come. Your working integrity, your conduct, your relational ship abilities, your emotional quotient and an entire host of soft skills are vital for profession achievement.

****

Enrich your Interpersonal skills

In today's workplace, having a particular skill is not adequate. You need to go past the typical skills and show what it takes to fit within the Organization. It is about working with different people. An ability to exist together with others while performing the occupation. Trademark traits like great behaviour, character, empathy, propensity, and appearance which help us to pass on and keep up a relationship with others are important. Interpersonal skills are the skills we make use of each day to impact and collaborate with other individuals, both exclusively and in groups. Individuals who have chipped away by creating solid interpersonal skills are typically more fruitful in both their professional and in their personal lives.

Bosses frequently try to hire staff with a solid interpersonal skill as they need individuals who will function admirably in a group and have the capacity to discuss successfully with associates, clients, and customers.

Interpersonal skills are not only essential in the work environment but also in our own and social lives can likewise be profited by better Skills. Individuals with greater interpersonal aptitudes are generally seen as idealistic, quiet, certain and alluring - qualities that are frequently charming and are natural in engaging others.

We have the various ways of interaction on communications. What we say and how we say it is Verbal

Whereas Non-Verbal Communication is what we convey without words.

Listening Skills - How we decipher both the verbal and non-verbal messages sent by others. Defining Negotiation, the most vital interpersonal skill which can diffuse conflict, here working with others to discover a common result. Problem Solving Issues is about tenaciously working with others to distinguish and tackle long-standing issues. Basic leadership in Decision making is exploring and examining choices to settle on sound choices. Confidence: The implied way of Communicating your qualities, thoughts, convictions and sentiments.

Here we discuss appearance. The first Impression is very imperative, they can be about the state of mind and in addition the dress you wear. The visual effect is at any rate as important as a verbal effect, individuals will rapidly make presumptions in light of your outward appearances on the attire you wear, how all around prepped up you are and how vibrant is your body language.

Seldom is it possible to adjust your face yet it should be possible about the appearance that is on it! However the day began and whatever minor issues have surfaced has en route, individuals have not come to see you with a dull look all over. It is your obligation to yourself and in addition to the organization that you appear to pass on a quiet, amicable and proficient outside, notwithstanding how you may feel inside. Attempt to smile and seem idealistic.

Intervention is a technique by which individuals settle conflicts. It is a procedure by which compromise or understanding is reached to maintaining a strategic distance from incongruity and dispute. In any contradiction, people understandably plan to accomplish an ideal result for their position or maybe an association they speak to. Be that as it may, the standards of equanimity, looking for a common advantage and keeping up a relationship are the keys to an effective result.

Negotiation skills are of various types that are employed in foreign affairs, in the judiciary, the government, Industrial disagreement or domestic conflict. Be that as it may, in general, negotiation can be learned and connected in an extensive variety of exercises and practicing this skill can be of incredible advantage in settling any disputes that emerge amongst you and others.

A misconception may be a valid reason for misfiring in Negotiation table. Such breakdowns tend to happen because of disparity of perspective, background or cultural propensity and also numerous other factors. In negotiation, it is conceivable not to listen what others mean to the state because of the absence of decisiveness with respect to the participating individual or futile consideration. Numerous professional negotiators will look forward what are known as a Win-Win situation. This includes solving solutions that permit both sides to benefit. In other words, negotiators plan to cooperate with other negotiating person or a group towards finding an amicable result for their disputes and disparities that result in both sides being fulfilled.

Problem-solving and Decision-making, everyone can gain by having problem-solving skills as we as a whole experience issues once a day; some of these issues are clearly more serious or complex than others. It is great to be able to tackle all issues effectively and in a convenient manner without trouble, lamentably, there is no particular way is available in which all the issues can be settled.

On the face of it, problem-solving as a subject is very perplexing. However well prepared we are for problem-solving there is a component of the obscurity that may likely to creep in. The spite of the fact is, planning and structuring the agenda will make the problem-solving process more prone to be fruitful, decision-making ability and a component of good fortunes will at last figure out if the problem solving was a success.

All problems have two characteristics in common; the Objectives and Hindrances.

Objectives: Issues include embarking to accomplish some goal or fancied situation and can incorporate keeping away from a circumstance or occasion. Objectives can be anything that you wish to accomplish, where you need to be. The objective may fluctuate accordingly. The CEO, the fundamental objective may not be same as others, it might be part into various sub-objectives keeping in mind the end goal to satisfy a definitive objective of lasting benefits.

Hindrances: In the event that there were no boundaries in the method for accomplishing an objective, then there would be no issue. Problem-solving includes manoeuvrings the blocks or snags that keep away the quick accomplishment of objectives.

Decision Making and self-confidence: We have come across many Individuals say that they think that it's difficult to decide. Dismally, we as a whole need to settle on choices constantly, running from inconsequential issues like what to have for lunch, straight up to life shifting issues like what to study, career change or even choosing a bride/bridegroom. A few people put off settling on choices, but unendingly hunt down for more information or getting other individuals involved supporting their proposals. Others turn to decision making by taking a vote, putting a stick in a rundown or flipping a coin.

In the simplest terms, decision making revolves around the two course of action one is by a) Intuition 2) Reasoning. Here intuition is utilizing your 'hunch or gut feeling' about conceivable strategies. Despite the fact that individuals discuss it as though it is a mystical wisdom, instinct is really a blend of past understanding and your own character. It merits considering your inner sense since it mirrors your finding out about existence. It is, in any case, not generally in view of reality, just your discernments, huge numbers of which may have begun in youth and may not have matured exceptionally.

Reasoning; this thinking utilizes the facts of available data before you to decide. Reasoning has its underlying foundations of being indistinct and the data might have been conceived recently. It can be that as it may, disregard emotional angles to the choice, and specifically, issues from the past that may influence the way that the choice is actualized. Intuition is considered to be a worthy method for settling on a preference, despite the fact that it is, for the most part, more fitting when the choice is a straightforward or should be made speedily. More entangled decisions have a tendency to require a more formal, structured approach, for the most part including both intuition and reasoning. It is essential to be careful about hasty responses to a circumstance.

Being assertive is a critical feature of developing interpersonal skills. Being decisive can help us to feel better about ourselves enhancing self-confidence. Many a time when we react, others can make us feel incompetent, liable or apologetic. These might be indications of indifferent behaviour. We may likewise feel irritated and disapproving of others amid conversation- this might be an indication of more aggression.

While honing assertiveness, it is imperative to recollect what assertiveness is and its significance in the communication mechanism. Being assertive is not the same as being aggressive; in actuality, assertiveness implies supporting what you have accepted. Assertiveness is expressing your considerations, feelings, convictions and conclusions in a genuine and a fitting way. As confidence have to be energized in others it is additionally vital to recall that we should consistently regard the deliberation, emotions, conclusion and convictions of other individuals.

Assertiveness permits people to state their own rights without undermining the privileges of others. It is viewed as a balanced reaction, being neither being passive or aggressive, with self-confidence playing a huge role. An assertive individual reacts as an equivalent to others and expects to be open in communicating their desires, contemplations, and emotions.

Take Away: Interpersonal skills are basic to creating other key life skills. Developing this skill will be able to communicate well with others, it is considered a basic skill in tackling issues that definitely happen both in our private and professional lives. It can cultivate powerful communication at a workplace. It can likewise open up numerous proficient ways and can keep up your social awareness.

There is an assortment of skills that can help you to prevail in the various arena of life and Skills you need has areas covering huge numbers of these. With regard to, the establishments of some different skills are based on only strong interpersonal skills since these are significant to our own personal relationship, socializing, and profession. Without great interpersonal skills, it is frequently harder to create other important soft or technical skills.

****

Communication skill is paramount.

Communication skills are ranked 1st among a job candidate's 'must have' skills and qualities. Why communication is so demanding? Communication has become an authentic platform between peers, managers and executives to share information be it the work place or a domiciliary environment. Basic communication skills is to distinguish who the listeners are, show respect, give concise delivery and use an appropriate modulation of voice, *the basic skills are* speaking, listening, reading and writing.

Experts opine communication is a complex process in which many possibilities for misapprehension and subsist. When communication is comprehensible everything is pellucid. We do come across many instances many of the employees in MNC'S are attracting pink slips due to either misperception or due to lack of communication.

Let us examine two different scenarios, have you ever sought the help of your colleague to intervene in an ongoing negotiation, instances where someone has helped you in re drafting a mail to your client. What went wrong in these situations? It may have been due to a breakdown in communication. In the workplace, you spend a lot of time interacting with peers. Peers are colleagues who are in a similar category as you are, usually in the same cadre, or who share a similar level of experience and expertise. Introspect, as the colleague stepped in the negotiation and the reply to the client mail fall in its place. Why was he able to when you were in want? Even though these two models are different, one has to read what's the common thread? They need to communicate to work together most effectively.

What exactly is communicating? John Maxwell defines it as the "ability to identify with people and relate to them in a way that increases your influence with them". John Maxwell is a leadership development expert and he's so passionate about communication that he wrote an entire book about it called "Everyone Communicates Few Connect". It's important to remember that while communication is focused on the way we speak to others and the words we use, it is also the way you use our body language. Body language can put forth a message equally as one delivered by words. Sometime written communication also has a hidden emotion. One can easily understand the passive aggression, disenchantment, and bias, in the way it is expressed.

In the history of humanity, written communication is a recent phenomenon. Initially, Communication existed in various forms since Homo sapiens appeared in this Planet. The methods, however, consisted of a muddled set of signs that could have different meanings to each human using them. It was only after Cognitive evolution humans were facilitated to speak. Even today signs and symbols are used to communicate with the masses which are a much understood communiqué than other forms of communication. Poor communication skills may lead to a lot of misunderstandings and bad personal relationships. This can cause stress and complications into one's life that will bring down greatly in the long run. One should avoid this at any cost!

<u>Non Verbal Communication</u>:

Nonverbal communication is the transmission of information in addition to words in a communication. The prime aspect of Non Verbal Communication is the body Language , This is studied by the way a person sits; stands; moves arms, hands, and feet; other subtle movements.

Facial expressions convey how someone feels about entity. These are used to show anger, grief, happiness, contempt, fear and confusion, among other feelings. Human faces are incredibly expressive including the eyes, eyebrows, mouth, and any other movement. Emotions such as anger, happiness, hurt, and boredom are all easily expressed with facial movements.

Good posture is an easy and very important way to maintain a healthy mind and body. When you practice correct posture, your body is in alignment with itself. This can alleviate common problems such as back or neck pain, headaches, and fatigue. How you carry yourself including bearing, stance, rigidity, uprightness. Whether you are leaning back comfortably, sitting rigidly on the edge of your seat, or leaning back with your eyes close, you convey a message through your posture and positioning.

Eye contact: focusing your eyes helps you concentrate. When your eyes wander, they take in random, extraneous images that are sent to your brain, slowing it down. When you fail to make eye contact with your listeners, you look less authoritative, less believable, and less confident. People often attribute trustworthiness to people who speak while maintaining good eye contact and vice versa. Eye contact is also used to convey interest and emotions, and to promote rapport with the receiver of the message. It is also used to feign interest, mislead, and fake interest.

Gestures differ from physical non-verbal communication that does not communicate specific messages especially hand gestures are rich conveyors of communication. They punctuate the spoken word and add meaning. Less conscious gestures such as scratching your nose, stroking your hair, tugging on your clothes, placing your hands on your hips, and waving communicate messages advertently or inadvertently.

In 1620, Juan Pablo de Bonet published the first book that taught sign language to the deaf. His writings were based on the work of an Italian physician, Girolamo Cardano, stated "hearing words were not necessary for understanding ideas". Signs and other articles with words, pictures or symbols are considered to be communicative.

Attire: Attire role is very significant, a doctor, advocate, are easily identifiable by their clothing. Types of clothing and your appearance send powerful nonverbal messages. Some of the messages are intentional as when the fan wears a shirt with his favourite IPL team emblazoned on the back.

Modern day Miscommunication: Today, the world is behind social media, huge populace uses this format of communication, but it proved to be a disaster for a salesman. The manager pinged the salesman as to find out has he given the quote to the client. The salesman in his exuberance typed "Y" instead of "S".The ego stricken manager found fault with the salesman concluded that salesman is challenging him by asking why, In this case , the salesman's intention did not convey his message; he was fired for no reason.

Oral Communication, This stratum of communication allowed information and comprehension to be transformed from an individual to group, from generation to generation. It also allows for the aggregation of knowledge through anecdotes, history of our civilization. This process began only by mouth. Long before writing was developed, groups of people carried stories to teach the young and to preserve the history. Let's appreciate our Neurological functioning of our brain. The Broca's area is the motor speech area and it helps in movements required to produce speech. Wernicke's area is the sensory area. It helps in understanding speech and using the correct words to express our thoughts. One has to know these important functions if they are curious to know how communication is processed in our brain.

How to improve our communication skills: Be aware, do practice, have a handwritten note for small talk, and try to remember points. Small talk is an art that not many people have mastered. Secondly is storytelling, I make sure all my training session will have 2 or 3 stories related to the subject. Stories are powerful. They activate our brains, make presentations attentive and interesting, and make us more persuasive. Everyone's got at least one great story in them.

A husband gets into an argument with his wife and they quarrel. They decided not to Communicate, but suddenly husband realized that he has to catch the morning flight and needed to wake up early. So he decided to write in a piece of paper a message to his wife" Please wake me up by 5AM".But when he woke up it was 9am.Furious why his wife has not woke him up he went in search, but to find only a note from his wife, "please wake up it is 5 AM". The pun here is, Husband cannot outsmart wife in effective communication.

Practicing Empathy while communicating; Communication is a two-way street. If you practice taking the opposing viewpoint, you can reduce the difficulty and anxiety that sometimes arises. Developing empathy helps you better understand even the non verbal aspect of your communication with others, and help you respond more effectively.

Next Important communication skill is writing skills .Good writing skills will propel you to communicate your message with clarity and reach to an audience than through facial or telephone conversations. Another way to improve your writing skills is to read through Audio Visual Mode, as you read, see and hear you pick up new vocabulary and engage with different writing styles.

We sum it up by expressing, try to adapt to whatever situation you find yourself in and make the other person feel comfortable and valued their conversation with you. By bettering verbal, non-verbal, and written communication skills, you can become more successful in all areas of business. Empathy is a necessary skill for you to master if you want to be successful with the current trend of communication skills.

****

Being Intelligent Emotionally.

In this quick paced life, not a day goes without enthusiastic annoy. Be it street seethe, shouting at the accomplice, family, losing auto keys, the unending ringing of cell phones, and irritating sounding among others. A large number of them are not in any case mindful they are enduring, as they imprudently draw in Negative Emotions.

In my two decades experience of meeting and collaborating with individuals, it has translucently uncovered the enthusiastic inadequacies in a significant number of them. In any case, I specify two of my dear companions, one who stood first in School, an XLRI and another, an ACA (Inter).Both oversaw exceptionally well in their scholastics and in the basic on unfurling a praised profession, yet two of them tumbled off in their vocations and lives. It was surprising to these folks, to respond in the drive of feelings.

It was glaring the IQ had impelled them to perform in their assiduity however their EQ has bombed horribly. At the point when everybody trusts it is an IQ which is the establishment for a valorous vocation, it is similarly vital to have it reinforced by a fit EQ.IQ may discover its foundations with Nature (DNA) though Emotional insight can be encouraged and educated. Feelings must be tended to sagaciously. Understanding feeling and taking care of it with adequacy is the centre of this theory, Emotional Intelligence.

Moving toward Emotional Intelligence through different domains like knowing your feelings being apprehension or love, gaging is expected to judge your fearlessness, ie mindfulness. Self Management is overseeing and aura of your feelings as per your quality and shortcoming, primarily seeing your rash impulse.

The fundamental benchmark of EQ guess is the Social awareness. Here you assess your feelings as well as conjecture the feelings of others. A few applicants were approached to assemble for an arrangement group discussion, there were total disquietude until a competitor approached to proffer, made everybody sit and stay tranquil. The employer which was watching this was Conscious to offer the placement for the possibility for his social mindfulness. As per EQ specialists "IQ gets you employed, yet EQ gets you advanced".

Having a clear understanding of your thought and behaviour patterns helps you understand other people. This ability to empathise expedites better personal and professional relationships. Knowing more about social issues makes us culpable and enables us to take efficient actions in concurrence to the society. Every responsible person in the society need to bring in the awareness among the school, college kids, to carry out their tasks very astutely and not to be exploited in any terms. This becomes mandatory for all of us after many episodes in the recent past.

In this present young men and young ladies don't vary much in their lead, both resorts to social tribulations, wherein young ladies are intentionally snared for sexual manhandle. Preparing kids about common sense, and convey them to the comprehension on the shades of malice of mishandling parental opportunity, will profit them develop into capable citizens of tomorrow. It will likewise help them to take well-thought choices.

I am forced to remember the discourse of US President Barack Obama in 2008 "there is a compassion insufficiency in the general public" it is valid. The greater part of the Kids invest their free energy in Mission Impossible, Pokémon, Coma, Candy squash, add up to etc.Society is innovation driven. It is a worldwide marvel; the more youthful are unaware of Empathy. The social media, online networking are being rebuked for this, there again not all posts on the

Face book are shared or enjoyed by even companions, and they oppose this idea.

The Social awareness will know the negative impacts of innovation and along these lines; it will direct the utilisation of innovation. Inspiration and Empathy for ethical glue, rehearsing it will acquire colossal social nobility. Then again, the part of Empathy in Corporate is of the distinctive measurement by and large. A large portion of the administrators feels that empathy might be dogmatized. This may not be truthful, there must be a blueprint. Feeling for somebody attempting to comprehends their perspective and it doesn't justify you to concur with their perspective. Managers empathising ought to be assertive, yet require need not be aggressive.

The vibe, values you declare and the objectives you reserve identifies with mindfulness. Managing how to conquer anger, upset, insecurity and self-assuredness ascribe to your certitude. Adapting to stress and feeling is the variable of poise. It is for certain this perspective similar in directing intrapersonal relationship among all. With every one of these viewpoints, de-focusing on stands tall in the quick needs of today.EQ can express this with adequacy.

Utilising EQ to de-stress

41

By rapidly quieting, calming down and pacifying stress helps you remain attuned, centred, and in control regardless of whatever dispute you face or however distressing a circumstance gets to be. Build up your anxiety, stress busting abilities by working these means: The initial step to lessening stress sees what feels like. How your body does respond when you're focused? Is your encountering tremor in your stomach, palpitation in your heart? Are your hands scrunched? Is your breath shallow? Monitoring your physical reaction to stress will help accommodate strain when it happens.

Isolate your stress reaction. Every individual responds diversely to stress. On the off chance that you have a tendency to wind up distinctly irate or fomented under anxiety, your best reaction is stress-easing exercises that quieted you down. In the event that you have a tendency to end up distinctly discouraged or pulled back, you will react best to push easing exercises that are empowering. If you tend to freeze in some ways while backing off from others, all you require is calming exercises that give both solace and incitement. Our framework isn't customised to be in flight or flight mode.

Find the stress-busting tenor that work for you. An ideal approach to lessen stress rapidly is by connecting with at least one of your five senses: Sight, sound, smell, taste, and touch. Every individual reacts indiscernible to tangible information, so you have to discover things that are assuaging or renewing to you. For instance, in case you're a visual individual, you can soothe worry by encircling yourself with advancing pictures. Visit a beautiful locale ideally with waterfalls. Having identified you react more to sound, you may discover a wind chime installed in your living place, a most loved bit of music at home or be tuning into music, either yester years Elvis Presley, Boney M, or Indian Classy of Lata, Burmans, Kishore kumar, Md Rafi, AR Rahman, Mastreo Ilayaraja, or empower your olfactory faculties related to fragrance by noticing blossoms ,agarbathis and rapidly decrease your stress levels. These go far in dealing with your worry through EQ.

Take Away: Creating emotional intelligence awareness requires significant time-consuming process and responsibility, however having a strong EQ is currently a vital quality for professional achievement. Luckily, you can take in the abilities of emotional intelligence and start applying them in your work environment immediately. As you do, you'll see a shift in the attitude of seniors and associates react to you.

The advantages of being candidly smart to add to individual accomplishment, in instruction, business and every single other circle of life.EQ assumes an extremely crucial part in Change Management. So let this general public, particularly the adolescent take in the significance of EQ, so they evade enthusiastic cordon and disregard radical choice bringing on passionate clamour. Give us all a chance to be energised and make our stay on this planet a euphoric experience.

****

Resolving Conflict

"Happiness is not the absence of conflict but the ability to resolve it effectively"

All of us do experience some form of conflict in our personal life. As a matter of fact, no two people on this planet agree, they end up stepping on each others' shoes during the course of any exchange of ideas. Conflict inherently is difficult to resolve. Though it is the method of restraining the negative aspects of conflict while increasing the positive aspects, it is seldom consumed by stakeholders easily. The focus on conflict management is to enhance learning, study group outcomes, including effectiveness or performance in an organizational setting. An objective of this article is to portray the different types of conflict, identify the sources of conflict and clarify the levels of conflict.

Let us presume the HRM and the GM of an MNC meet for the upcoming agenda to draft a presentation to the CEO and come up with numerous views. Every reflection is carefully examined by both even if it is conflicting to their personal ideas and they present it to the superior for final adjudication. Constructive conflict is the most effective conflict situation that you can encounter. It encourages the expression of opinions in a controlled and respectful manner. The constructive conflict also sets the stage for healthy conflict and for resolution. It also encourages growth and innovation.

On the Contrary, if the HRM insists his/her ideas to be implemented and overrules the suggestions of the GM, destructive conflict ensues. And this is an unhealthy environment, which controls thoughts and does not empower those for alternative ways of thinking. This allows issues from a personal perspective to get in the way of controlling an environment, and it causes more destructive behaviour. It is toxic.

Daniel Katz' theories of Destructive Conflict divide the source of conflict into three categories, Economic, Value, and Power. Economic conflict is basically a situation where the resources are in short supply. These sources can be many different things, they can be human resources, office supplies, budget, social loafing, they can be displayed fixtures or company products.

When the sources are scarce in an organisation, the employees tend to hoard these resources, as they never know when the access to these resources will become available. So, you might find individuals, in reality, watching and waiting for resources and are not made available to them by their team members. They will not provide their team with the support necessary by sharing the resources that they've hoarded. This is clearly an enervated behaviour when this practice takes place; it is the additional conflict between the teams, peers and managers.

Value conflict is between ideals, and principles, and preferences. This is very difficult to sort out between individuals because values are something that all carry to the work environment. Many individuals in the work environment may mirror the values of the organisation, and some of the values that the individuals hold very dear may be contradictory to what the environment supports.

So when individuals bring their own personal values into the work environment and expect other individuals to behave within their definition of values, a conflict can result. For the reason that as you can envisage, not everyone follows the same set of values. So if these values, principles or preferences are taken to the extreme, where individuals expect everyone to behave such as they do, believe such as they do, or follow the same philosophies such as they do. You'll have discord and it'll be a source of conflict. You can always find disagreement among the members arising out of state political allegiance.

Power and control are other interesting factors in destructive conflict. When you think about power and control; you may imagine an individual you've worked with on a team, in a department or maybe in a division. Power is very obsessive to some individuals. Power is something that some people believe to be identified who they are. Maybe a designation possibly is in charge of over a team or a project, pleading for a power position can be counterproductive, and then this course causes destructive conflict.

Workplace Conflicts

We come across various instances where employees find a conflict of Interest.

a)   An employee working part-time for a competitor.

b)   An employee accepting free gifts and free products from Vendor.

c)   Male Manager coercing a female employee who reports to him.

Let's take a team setting, where an individual takes the power in always being the first to speak. Overpowering individuals in a dialogue are enforcing their situation or their position or their decision to the rest of the team. It can also happen when an individual is dominant or control of a work unit where no one's appointed them for this position. But they've decided to be the one that does take the lead role even though it's not supported by anybody else on the team. Power is something that's very common in a work environment and I'm sure you've experienced it and have already experienced the source of conflict that it can cause.

Interpersonal conflict is between individuals. So, it can be something that is specific to two individuals, not necessarily a whole team. So, maybe it is a situation where two individuals just don't get along, or they can't seem to have a civil conversation. It can be something that they have brought to the work environment. When individuals bring interpersonal issues to the work environment, conflict not only exists between the two of them but it also can be very dysfunctional for the team that they work in.

And it's been a long time since they've been able to. So, if this type of behaviour is allowed to exist, conflict ensues, and it's a perfect example of destructive conflict. When you're talking about the levels of conflict, the role is also something that is very important. If the roles are not defined clearly between the team members, as to who is the leader or the followers, who are the peers, who are the decision makers, or who the resources go to, one will have issues with the level of conflict.

If I don't know whom you have to go to for decisions, then no decisions are made. This can not only be between individuals, it can be between groups and divisions as well. So defining roles in a team is more than just applying a title to an individual. It's actually outlining the responsibilities and the position that they play within the team. Another level of conflict can be intergroup. So it can be two divisions or groups of people that might be fighting for resources. Might be fighting over who's playing which role in a project.

Professor Ms, Najila Debow, University of California, Irvine lecturing on Conflict resolution skills explicates "when it becomes intergroup, you can have issues with respect to marketing and sales. They could be fighting over who's responsible for the lack or generation of a sales volume. Is it the sales team? Or is it the marketing group that isn't providing the sales team with the right materials", to sell the product, which then, of course, affects the revenue. So Intergroup is very critical to ensure that groups don't become siloed and only interest in their own success or their own performance.

You have to really think about cross-functional teams in order to ensure that this level of conflict does not exist.Multi-party, it's between companies. It can also be thought of as mergers and acquisitions. When you bring in a new company into an organisation, it can be very critical in determining how a company is going to be absorbed into the parent organisation. Individuals, when mergers and acquisitions happen.

If they are the surrendering party, then it's very personal to them. They can have a history that they bring that maybe they've been with the organisation for a ten year period of time, and they don't like the idea that this is happening. There's a lot of emotion that goes on through this time and you can have a lot of conflicts that ensues (Bank of Madura & ICICI). It also can be value driven. So it can also, quite frankly, be economic. So when you're looking at levels of conflict and focusing on multi Bank, or the example that we're giving, mergers and acquisitions.

It's very important to understand the levels of conflict that can play in this type of action and to ensure that you at least acknowledge that this can take place. Intercultural conflict is something that is expanding in our workplace for two reasons. We have a very diverse workforce and, two because most companies are global and they're interfacing on a global trail. So when you're looking at inter-cultural conflict. It's more complex, and it will take a more text describing it. Let us look into resolving these conflicts;

I am reminded of the famed narrative depicting conflict resolving. An Arabian dad left behind in "will", of all his holdings, half to be given his elder son second son gets one-third and third one ninth. But the dad left 17 camels as his asset. Conflict surfaced between sons as they could not divide the will* in the said ratio. An expert was pressed into service, he immediately swung into action. He asked the sons to take his solitary camel also into the kitty. Now the total became 18, he gave the first son 9 camels, second son 6 camels and the third son 2 camels, the total came to 17, he took back the camel he gave. It necessitates an intellectual attitude to resolve this conflict.

There are several modes of diffusing conflict; the time tested method is active listening and intervention. You have to initially identify conflict and should prepare yourself when to do an appropriate intervention. Applying listening is the core for Conflict management. Active listening prescribes using effective communication which is a powerful force to your advantage. Intervention from a status viewpoint may not diffuse conflict. Translating complaints and criticism into request with a positive outcome, this can be applied for yourselves and for the stakeholders.

Maintaining respect among your work group and to all employees will be an easy entrée when conflict escalates. The employees should be aware of their roles, responsibilities and limitations. Unexpected organisational change can be a ground for conflict. As an administrator envisaging unforeseen exigencies can lessen conflict.

Kumar Mehta and Ravi Agarwal are chosen by the management to be project managers. They have the ability to work well with each member and have achieved the given agenda much ahead of time and within the budget. Their merits were analysed and asked why and what way they excelled. Many felt they were good communicators and they listen actively dealt their issues effectively. They never complained, they put everything to request. They are respectful to each other. They keep their roles and responsibilities very clear. They were very mindful in effecting a change.

Take Away: Conflict resolution is key to any life situation be at home, occupation, social gathering or sports activities. It is mandatory that higher level of Communication is needed to understand and participate in the efforts necessitating for positive Conflict resolution. Through your natural styles, you will be able to strengthen your Communication, identifying the best approach reviewing the facts of the conflict, using these skills to establish a collaborative approach and discovering the options important for resolution. It may be deterrent to have controls of all variables while seeking diffusion. It ultimately boils down on how you react to ease the tension, challenge yourselves and utilise these new found skills to increase your effectiveness in resolving a conflict.

Conflict resolution permits individuals to move past their own particular feelings and suppositions to score on target choices. By following these skills in the working environment, you empower a more profound comprehension of circumstances that emerge from the other individuals in the workplace. Employees figure out how their associates feel and think, and also how to collaborate with them. The stakeholders who are involved investigate the circumstance and consider other conceivable solution to strife.

****

A perfect Leader..

Deriving from various classifications, these definitions seem to be more appropriate to delineate a Leader "a person who influences a group of people towards the achievement of a goal. A leader by its meaning is one who goes first and leads by example, so that others are motivated to follow him. This is a basic requirement. To be a leader, a person must have a deep-rooted commitment to the goal that he strives to achieve, even if nobody follows him".

As a leader, one has to understand who he is and what strengths he possesses in order to influence the behaviour of his followers. This starts by performing an analysis of the strengths weaknesses and setting goals that put the skills to real test. In abstract, one must expect more from himself than expecting from its followers; this is how many followers get motivated from the one who leads from the front. By having certain skills and using them appropriately, you become a leader among your colleagues, start developing such skills to become the best at what you are. You will then find it possible to set milestones for your followers.

Ultimately, it is the actions that influence the amount of drive that your followers are going to have. If you have a vision, which you don't seem to nurture you are likely to de-motivate your followers. On the contrary, if vision is translated into action, you lead by example to perform activities, which people want to emulate then it becomes vibrant.

Let us explore the different traits of leadership

Vision

Standing firm when it comes to the policies and procedures is all well and good, but it doesn't speak to having a vision. As a leader, you have to learn to communicate your vision or the vision to your followers. But how can you do that? Learn to paint a picture with words. Speak it, write it, draw it, and touch it. Whatever methods you can use to create a picture, do it. As they say, "A picture is worth a thousand words."Ask each of the other team managers in your company to tell you, in their own words, about the vision of the company. How close is it to what you thought they understood? Is your team on the same page as you?

As you work, your company's vision should be in your mind every day, and you should revaluate it occasionally so that it stays current with the changing times in which we live. And be mindful, your staffs need to be as involved as you in keep it up to date if you truly want them follow your vision. Be sure to keep your key players involved.

In our Leadership training program we used this methodology to drive the Vision into the participants. Various groups were formed and a group had 5 participants, they were given a Chart with Colour felt pen. They have to visualize their goal, and make an inventive depiction; most of them came up with an innovative creative percipience.

"It's not the man that makes the vision; it's the vision that makes the man." - Mahatma Gandhi. Here a mention about Mahatma Gandhi would be fitting, though his vision on India's freedom was highly unorthodox. He galvanized his followers to participate and connect to freedom struggle without bloodshed.

Passion

When you talk about your vision for the company, let your passion for your vision shine through. Others will feel it and want to get on board with you. If you don't have passion for your vision, you need to recreate your vision or reframe your description of your vision so it's connected to your passion. It is important to find the areas you are passionate about then stay focused on them. Passion produces energy, vision, motivates others. Passion is such a key part of being a great leader that if you don't have it, you simply can't be a great leader. Think of all the great leaders throughout the ages and try to name one that did not have passion.

These days we cannot talk about success without mentioning Face book's CEO, Mark Zuckerberg. The 27-year old billionaire has changed the world we live in. One of these ingredients is he followed his passion - not money.

Decision making.

Some leaders have a set process, and others make decision unilaterally. But you don't want to be one of those leaders who consults no one before making a decision, announces the change the next day and then gets frustrated when no one follows it. If you're one of those, it is advised to implement a set process.

In fact, here's a system you can use to become a better decision maker. It's called the Q-CAT:

Q = Quick. Be quick but not hasty.

C = Committed. Be committed to your decision but not rigid.

A = Analytical. Be analytical, but don't over-analyze (Too much analysis can cause paralysis.)

T = Thoughtful. Be thoughtful about all concerned, but don't be obsessive.

A Study on Steve Jobs exemplary functioning reveals his decision making abilities. Apple was a successful company from 1976 to 1985, it almost failed in the mid-1990s. Apple survived because Steve Jobs learned how to adapt. He became a democratic/participative/charismatic leader, and Apple soared. Jobs combined and added several leadership styles, he hired other experienced leaders and entrusted them to excel. Jobs encouraged his lead designer to bring in a new blue print. That why Apple survived.

Be a team builder.

To become a great leader, you must develop a great team or, one might say, a well serviced machine. But how do you do that? You can start by handing off responsibility to your team and letting your team to run with it. Don't breathe down their necks and don't micromanage, but make yourself available if questions or problems come up. Teach your team to use the Q-CAT decision-making system and give them the freedom to work through their own decisions. Don't forget to use humor to keep your team's spirits up during a crisis. When an emergency hits, your team will look up to you to be a tower of strength and endurance.

Mahendra Singh Dhoni was able to build a formidable team to empower ascendancy in all formats of the game. Under his unsullied leadership Indian Cricket was able to triumph the world cup for the second time and won the first 20; 20 Championship.

You must have character.

Without character, all the other "traits" are a fritter. That's because your innate character strengths and limitations play a critical role in your leadership style. The real question is, are you aware of just what role they play? All great leaders have taken steps to learn about their individual personality and what part it plays in their leadership style. Leaders are seen by their followers intrinsically; hence the character of a Leader is paramount.

Developing character

Some dimensions of character, specifically some traits, are inherited. Virtues, values and many other traits are developed during early childhood, and modified as a result of education, family influences, early role models, work and social experiences, and other life events. The early philosophers viewed character as something that is formed, subconsciously, through repetitive behavior that is either rewarded or by finding what works through experience.

K.Kamaraj Ex Chief Minister of Tamilnadu, he enlisted himself as a volunteer in the freedom movement, he was totally under the spell of Mahatma Gandhi and to the very end he remained Gandhian by conviction and practice. He portrayed enormous character as a Leader.

Having seen the traits of Leadership our focus now shifts to the style of Leadership. According to Daniel Golem an, he list out various styles of Leadership, six basic leadership styles:

1. Coercive leadership demands total and immediate compliance,

2. Authoritative leadership mobilizes people towards a common vision,

3. Affiliative leadership emphasizes harmonious working relationships,

4. Democratic leadership builds consensus through participation,

5. Pacesetting leadership expects excellence and self-direction, and

6. Coaching leadership seeks ways to develop employees.

The authoritative leadership style is the most effective of all six styles. A case study here will throw more light into this. Within a month of becoming the executive director at Education Unlimited (a non-profit that provides mentoring opportunities to low-income children), David Owings realized that the organization lacked direction. The next strategic planning session was still four months away, but David knew he had to do something immediately to remedy the smugness around him.

David decided to call a meeting of all employees to ask the question "what is it that we are truly about?" This resulted in a lively discussion in which employees concluded that, at its core, the organization was about inspiring young people to find their niche in society. As the example shows, the authoritative leader is a visionary who motivates people by helping them see how their work fits into a larger vision for the organization. People who work for such leaders understand that what they do matters and why. The problem is that not all leaders possess the ability to motivate and inspire.

Today world is filled up with Authoritative Leaders who inspires, to name a few, former USA President Barak Obama, Russian President Vladimir Putin, and Indian Prime Minister Narendra Modi. As far as internal India is concerned, Deceased Tamilnadu Chief Minister Ms. J.Jayalaitha stands distinctive in exercising her Leadership capabilities not only as an Authoritative Leader in terms of Governance but also scores in extending enormous welfare scheme to benefit the deprived.

Total Leadership

Let us further in looking at the Total leadership as discussed by Prof. Stewart d. Friedman, PhD, Wharton School University of Pennsylvania. He finds that integrating the character of Leadership in the four domains mentioned below, can only position you as a total leader. He rollouts the domains as 1) Work 2) Home 3) Society 4) Self. Scoring four-way wins starts by taking a clear view of what you want from and can contribute to each domain of your life, now and in the future, with thoughtful consideration of the people who matter most to you and the expectations you have for one another. Professor explains on what a good life can be and he suggests,

1) Be Real: Act with Authenticity, from **Fake, unfocused, rootless** acting with Authenticity by clarifying what's important, genuine, and Purposeful.
2) Be whole; From fragmented, resentful, Overwhelmed, Act with Integrity by respecting Person and stay connected, supportive and resilient
3) Be innovative: from being stagnant, apathetic, pessimistic, be innovative, act with creativity by experimenting how things get done more effectively. Leaders be Curious, engaged and optimistic. Summing total leadership

Distribute your time, if you are spending more hours in the office, you have to dedicate more time for your family at least in the weekend. The society and self plays a most important role, as you are a part of this society spend time once in a month by participating and contributing your skills, knowledge to the community by engaging in some social activity. The most important aspect is self, many of them leave this domain unattended, resulting in attracting unnecessary propensity, make sure you practice daily renewals for up keeping your mental serenity and robust health. Thus we conclude by toting up communion of these domains brings in a total perpetual Leadership.

Why is Change irrefutable?

Charles Darwin mollified "It is not the most grounded species that survive, nor the shrewdest: it is the one most versatile to change". Be that as it may, intentionally, Change is not generally welcome. Change Management dislike dealing with the execution of another IT framework, where you can physically observe distinctive equipment and programming, despite the fact that that may in itself be a piece of a change administration activity. Change is consistent. Our Red platelets are changed inside 120 days. Within 12 years our whole skeleton experiences a change and new bones are supplanted. There are trillions of cells which shrink and crisp cells are framed.

Managing change more often than not comes down to convincing individuals to act especially or diverse way, whether that is working with new hardware, inside another structure or with an alternate arrangement of procedures. It thoroughly considers what you are doing and why you are doing it in as most ideal as. In the event that you do that, you will be better ready to keep away from the pitfalls and, all the more decidedly, the clearer the photo you have of what you are attempting to accomplish and the more you will have the capacity to pick up the dedication of others to your arrangements.

We are cannoned by penchants, are a run of the mill part of every individual's lives, in any case, it is as often as possible counterproductive when overseeing change. As individuals, we are terrible at advancing. We contradict change. We consider changes to be a negative thing, something that makes dubiousness and shakiness. Changes must be recognized soundly.

Undoubtedly, even in our regular errands, we find our self-open to embarking to a comparable shop, whether it is an essential need to a salon. We are not inclined to change or recognize the change. A conventional change management gets ready, routinely progresses different negative mental states, this is an issue of first significance highlight to restrict change is Denial, here we fight the change and guarantee the standard.

Exactly when this is backing we are subjected to frustration and shock: when we comprehend that we can't avoid the change and we get the opportunity to be timid because of an absence of care. We endeavour diverse methodologies to back off or save this change by exchange and internal strife. In case all these disregards to inflame to conditions, where debilitation tries to find its bearing when we comprehend that none of the old ways can be joined into the new.

Right away we are objectively organized. Acceptance, so we a little bit at a time recognize the change, and start to set ourselves up. Likewise, after this, we try testing: where we endeavour to find new ways and ceaselessly oust the old limits. We have now found that change has the entire fragment to improve our future this accomplishment. The last is fusing the above-discussed point of view and keeping up this change. In any case, Organization Change is done at different levels through sorts of Changes.

Incremental change is the kind of progress that is seen happening through constant change. The means are little however over the time they get to be total and the change can be huge. A decent case of incremental change is an assembling organization making several parts that fit a bigger item, similar to an auto. Enhancing the assembling procedure of each of these essential segments each one, in turn, to cut expenses and enhance prepare productivity, by and large, is incremental change.

Mechanical or Technological Change

Mechanical change is a procedure of the creation, advancement, and scattering of innovation. The term is synonymous with innovative improvement, mechanical accomplishment, and innovative advance. In setting, Technological Change is the development of another innovation which is much less demanding to adjustment, the nonstop procedure of enhancing an innovation. To put it plainly, mechanical change depends on both better and more innovation incorporated into the system of existing operational procedures.

Apple has been an immense contributor to today's innovation. The innovation development of Apple began from the principal cutting edge PC then I Mac, I pad, I phone, I tunes. The starting of Apple App Store a year after the iPhone turned out changed the world into another experience. By this we perceive Steve Jobs perfect vision, today Apple has changed the innovation world.

Radical change, in any case, Change is exceptionally obvious. This kind of progress frequently comes about because of benchmarking or businesses prepare re-building practices and include a solitary critical stride change. Give us a chance to inspect the instance of IBM CEO Lou Gerstner. In 1983, IBM had $8 billion in debts and was almost bankrupt, Gerstner felt IBM had turned out to be excessively inflexible and incapable, making it impossible to change or adjust, and he begins changing the way of life to one of cooperation, inventiveness, and advancement. Gerstner encouraged collaboration among representatives and made the organization more clients centered. He did this by settling on intense choices, preparing the workers and demonstrating the conduct to achieve a transformational change.

Participative change depends on the goodwill of those included in the change to work through the change procedure. In worldwide associations, successful pioneers guarantee that groups work solidly. By directing workshops, preparing, and group building work out, these pioneers urge their subordinates to be more empathetic towards their associates, business accomplices, and providers. This practice mixes ability in managing diverse societies, traditions, and conventions; accordingly, compelling pioneers cultivate a synergistic work. A helpful change, be that as it may, is darker and not all that surely knew in the business.

Coordinated change depends on those rolling out the improvement having the ability to request others and to roll out the improvement to happen. It is an order by the holder of Power, or his approved operator, to roll out an improvement to the agreement. This is regularly finished with a work change mandate, a change arranges, or through notice. Jan Timmer previous CEO of Philips has earned the notoriety of sparing Philips from insolvency. How isn't he that right? To enhance the reality to the top official, and to make a feeling of proprietorship in them, he discharged a Hypothetical Press release on Company's Bankruptcy. This got the change the share expanded to 150% in 4 years. Having talked about the sorts of Change, we need to without a doubt comprehend alternate precepts of Change. These are advanced through standard and let us securitize them separately.

Diverse individuals respond distinctively to change. The change and soundness are the two inverse finishes off the range. Every individual differs in their objectives and their recognition. A security situated individual finds that conditions are changing quickly, or a change-arranged individual finds that everything is the same and there is just the same old thing new. In these circumstances, the people included can encounter disappointment, stress, and pessimistic states of mind towards people with inclinations at the flip side of the range.

Everybody has fundamental needs that must be satisfied: Psychologist Will Schultz recognized three essential needs that individuals have in interpersonal relations. These essential needs are additionally of key significance in individuals' response to change: The requirement for control, the requirement for inclusion, the requirement for openness, these necessities shift between individuals, in any change procedure there is constantly some level of control over one's predetermination.

Change endures misfortune, and one needs to experience that. This is exampled as Loss curve. We do encounter this incident; on the off chance that somebody who is junior gets advanced, or there is a sudden melancholy, this happens and it is abbreviated as "Sarah" bend, implies one experience Shock took after by outrage and afterward dismissal, in any case, capitulates to acknowledgment and the mending happens. There can be an underlying period where the change does not adjust in. Be that as it may, when the misfortune is acknowledged individual hits an amazing failure. The profundity of this "low" is extended if the misfortune is sudden or unforeseen. The time of change in accordance with the new circumstance can be exceptionally excruciating and take quite a while. On account of loss, the time of conformity can be the length of a couple of years.

Projections to be managed practically:

The relationship between projection and reality is very important. You can see this in customer relations, if a supplier fails to meet expectations then the customer is unhappy; if the supplier exceeds expectations then the customer is happy. My recent training tenure with Bankers was to highlight them on these grounds not to be over ambitious, extravagant resulting in overselling.

Dealing with Fear; this means that people often fear the worst; in fact, they fear far more than the worst, because their subconscious minds suddenly become illogical and see irrational consequences. Say, for instance, the company is reducing staff, which means, will I be shown the door. What happens to my family and my monthly bills? This will make people redundant. Such fears need to be addressed. Here is an interesting anecdote narrating how an eagle accepting changes to extend its occupancy in this planet.

EAGLE can live up to 70 years, but to reach this age, the eagle must make a hard decision in its' 40's.Its' long and flexible talons can no longer grab prey which serves as food, Its' sharp beak becomes bent because of aging and heavy wings, due to their thick feathers. It becomes stuck to its' chest and makes it difficult to soar.

Now the eagle is left with only 2 options: die or go through a painful process of change which will last 150 days. The process requires that eagle fly to a mountain and the eagle knocks its' beak against a rock until it collapses; eagle will wait for a new beak to grow back. When its' new talons grow back, the eagle starts plucking its' old-aged feathers and after 5 months, the eagle can take its' flight of rebirth and can further live for 30 more years.

Many times, in order to survive, we have to start a change process. We sometimes need to get rid of old memories, habits and other past traditions. On freeing from the past burden we can accept change. Let's all welcome change and embrace it, as change is a small step to evolution.

****

Mitigate Stress, Stay Relaxed.

Stress Management, the awareness on Stress need to be constituted among all, and this article will explore the causes, symptoms of stress, which is now considered to be a cause of erratic behaviour among young adults, and a silent killer among many adults. According to ISMA UK Stress defines as "that arises when the pressure placed upon an individual exceeds the capacity of that individual to cope. The adverse reaction people have to excessive pressures or other types of demand placed on them at work, those pressures may come from a number of different sources, and when their combined effect is overwhelming, stress occurs".

The major cause of stress in life is mostly family related. It may be a spouse, posterities. Family subjections and demands can be overwhelming. They include the delicate issue of finance; the relationship may turn turbulent leading to arguments, problems of closeness and communication, as well as the death of a loved one. Another area where we encounter stress is at the workplace. Sometimes work satisfaction is not there, compensation is not enough, you are not able to stand the boss, there is too much work to do, you feel frustrated and there are disagreements with colleagues.

Besides family and workplace, the stress can be experienced when you go through a traumatic experience. Experiences such as going through sexual abuse, an accident, violent break-in, surviving an earthquake, the flood can really take a toll on you. Psychological conditions can also cause a lot of stress. We are in the Era of Stress. And we should learn how to live with it. In this epoch of pressure, anxiety, performance, we are subjected with newer causes of stress being added every day; the list of stressors continues to augment. Coping strategies do work but to a limited extent. While the psychological phenomenon known as stress has only had a formal name for just over 80 years. The blitz of stress was discussed by our primogenitors much earlier. Even God Heads has given us suggestions on Combating Stress.

Stress Management starts with spotting the sources of stress in your life. Your true sources of stress aren't always understandable, and it's all too easy to overlook your own stress-inducing thoughts, feelings, and behaviours. Sure, you may know that you're constantly worried about work deadlines.

There are two kinds of stress: 1) good stress (Eustress) and, 2) Stress (Distress). Obviously, when talking about the negative impact of stress, research is referring to the distress. But it is important to note that humans need the stress. The challenge is to achieve the benefits that are gained from good stress and not to become overwhelmed by stress.

The three levels of stress are 1) Acute stress, the stress that arises from day-to-day interaction in the world that is due to some kind of conflict that is often temporary. American Psychological Association confides, "Everyday stressors can be managed with healthy stress management behaviors." However, when stress lasts for a prolonged period of time it becomes chronic and can lead to serious health problems".

Emotional distress — some combination of anger or irritability, anxiety and depression, the three stress emotions. Muscular problems, including a tension headache, back pain, jaw pain and the muscular tensions that lead to pulled muscles and tendon and ligament problems. The stomach is considered to be the 4th brain it reacts to stress, gut and bowel problems such as heartburns, acid stomach, flatulence, diarrhoea, constipation and irritable bowel syndrome. Transient over arousal leads to an elevation in blood pressure, rapid heartbeat, sweaty palms, heart palpitations, dizziness, migraine headaches, cold hands or feet, shortness of breath and chest pain.

2) Chronic stress (subordinate stress) – the result of an acute stressor such as a work related issue that goes on day in and day out (e.g., conflict with the boss) that wears at the person daily and puts them at risk for suffering the negative impacts of stress, such as stress-related illness.

Chronic stress (subordinate stress)

This is the grinding stress that wears people away day after day, year after year. Chronic stress destroys bodies, minds, and lives. It wreaks havoc through long-term attrition. People are immediately aware of acute stress because it is new; they ignore chronic stress because it is old, familiar, and sometimes, almost comfortable. Chronic stress kills through suicide, violence, heart attack, stroke and, perhaps, even cancer.

3) Traumatic stress – a stressor that is outside the person's normal coping skills, such as an accident or disaster. Traumatic events such as an accident or disaster, Loss of dear one, chronic illness or an accident. A stressor that is outside the person's normal coping skills. Shock and disbelief, you may have a hard time accepting the reality of what happened. Helplessness the sudden, unpredictable nature of natural disasters like accident, floods, and tremor may leave you vulnerable and helpless. The symptoms of traumatic stress are not just emotional they're also physical. There are various symptoms.

Psychological symptom; There may be no reason, but you will find Inability to concentrate or make simple decisions leading to memory breach. The tendency to become rather vague, easily distraught, less intuitive and creative, undue worrying, negative thinking, depression, anxiety, prone to accidents, Insomnia or waking tired.

 The emotional outburst is very common in our country, tearful scenes, Irritability, mood swings extra sensitive to criticism, defensive, feeling out of control, Practicing narcissism lack of motivation and drive, recurrent anger, highly frustrated, lack of confidence and lack of self-esteem.

Physical symptoms have a very long list to the impact of Stress. Aches spreading over the body, resulting in muscle spasm. With mounting tension, some tend to grind teeth. With stress being active frequent colds, infections are prone. Sometimes stress causes Allergies.

According to WebMD "Researchers followed 179 people with hay fever for 12 weeks and found that 39 percent of them had more than one flare-up. Those patients had higher levels of stress than those who didn't have allergy symptoms during the study period".

Rashes and skin irritations is a valid symptom of Physical Stress. Some suffer constipation or diarrhoea, the real cause of this is stress. Weight loss or gain, indigestion, acid reflux, heartburn, peptic ulcers is truly a symptom of Physical Stress. The thyroid hyperventilating lump in the throat, dizziness, pulsation, panic attacks, diabetes and nausea, physical tiredness, menstrual changes, her diabetes and High blood pressure are Physical symptoms of Chronic stress.

In this fast demanding world, only performance is adept, this has a cascading effect on the behaviour, not making enough time for relaxation or pleasurable activities but trying cover up Increased interdependence on alcohol or continuous smoking, but one may not be aware smoking might accelerate the stiffening of the large- to middle-sized arteries., caffeine excessive leads to insomnia, getting addicted to illegal drugs, becoming a workaholic, poor time management or poor standards of work absenteeism self-neglect , social withdrawal relationship problems recklessness , aggressive anger outbursts nervousness, Uncharacteristically lying.

Adaptation to Stressor

What cannot be cured has to be endured. If you can't change the stressor, change yourself. You can adapt to stressful situations and regain your sense of control by changing your expectations and attitude. Try to view stressful situations from a more positive perspective. Rather than fuming about a traffic jam, look at it as an opportunity to pause and regroup, listen to your favourite radio station, or enjoy some alone time. Look at the big picture. Take the perspective of the stressful situation. Ask yourself how important it will be in the long run. Will it matter in a month? A year? Is it really worth getting upset over? If the answer is no, focus your time and energy elsewhere. Keep asking "So what". Focus on the positive. When stress is getting you down, take a moment to reflect on all the things you appreciate in your life, including your own positive qualities and gifts. This simple strategy can help you keep things in perspective.

The Power of your positive mind and attitude is essential in translating stress to your advantage. Stress can be a motivator, if you're apprehensive because you have a big assignment due, this may motivate you to work on it and complete it. The stress can help you to put in your very best effort. If you're afraid of losing your job, stress may encourage you to raise your own standards and make improvements you most likely would not have done without the threat of unemployment. But many a time Stress is inconvenient. It gives room for health disorders like BP, Diabetic, tachycardia, and hypertension leading to heart Attack.

Learn to manage your time more effectively, we waste a lot of time doing unimportant tasks, especially when stressed, so prioritize your day and do the important jobs first. The unimportant ones can wait, and often they will disappear completely leaving you time to do other things. Also, do not put off the unpleasant tasks, avoidance causes a great deal of stress. Give unpleasant tasks a high priority and do them first.

How to Mitigate Stress;

My study in Mitigating Stress starts with <u>eating regimen</u>: If there is no abuse on eating routine, by and large there is no much scope for physical stress. Because of quick ways to life and the differing environment we are presented with an undesirable eating schedule. We have simple access to processed food, which is low-valued as well as contains loads of calories and destructive additives. Stress and contamination add to the negative impacts that tend to bolster your weight. Your weight is a straightforward equation of the amount you have eaten and drank; and the amount of that your body has used to fuel your physical exercises.

Less Calorie nourishment consumption and selective solid eating regimen appear to be an immaculate pitch to handle increasing body weight. Eat 3 regular balanced meals and 2 healthy snacks with plenty of water and juices every day. We are not aware, the most of the food we consume is acidic, Oil is acidic, and sugar is acidic. Less Ph in the system (acidic) absorbs all energy faster and leaves you very tired. Keeping the diet to neutral or alkaline is the best way to stay energetic throughout the day.

Rest

Sound sleep and stress tend to bring about an endless loop, in case you're anxious and stressed, then you can't rest, which makes you not well prepared to deal with the stressors of the following day, prompting to more flaring up of irritation and anger. To alleviate worry before bed, attempt some unwinding systems like profound breathing (Square Breathing) and separate from online networking an hour prior to sleep time. To guarantee the correct measure of sleep no less than 6-7 hours is exhorted until the inside purging is completed by Melatonin a very rich anti-oxidant.

Meditation & Exercise

A sound body and Healthy mind advocate the reinforcing of these two fundamental parameters which can relieve stress. Begin the morning with Meditation, Yoga. Take vigorous walking around minimum 45 minutes. This goes far in overseeing stress. Most of the corporate world over has added meditation (Emotional Intelligence) to their in-house training. As we might know meditation cleanses our mind and promotes calmness in us. It helps to mitigate stress and anxiety.

Quick cleansing

ISMA UK ;(International Stress Management Association UK) suggests 60-second Tranquilizer be relieved from Stress.

"The 60 Second Tranquillizers" This is a quick and easy breathing technique to bring about rapid relief when needed. Using positive thoughts will activate the parasympathetic nervous system and helps you to switch off your fight/flight reaction.

It is the perfect solution to rapidly calm nerves, focus the mind and help you to think more clearly. You can use this simple and powerful exercise at any time when you feel worried, tense, nervous or anxious. The benefit of this exercise is that it can be done anywhere and at any time. This can be done either sitting down or standing up; you may close your eyes if it is safe to do so or if you prefer keeping them open.

• Say firmly but silently to yourself – "take control".

Repeat – "I can do anything I want to" and breath out slowly.

• Slowly breathe in through your nose and then out through pursed lips, allowing the abdomen to soften and rise on the in the breath then deflate and return to normal on the out breath.

• Slowly repeat this for 6-8 breaths over the minute with the breath out being slightly longer than the breath in.

 • Say to you each time – "I am breathing in peace & blowing away tension".

• Each time you breathe out; make sure you relax your face, jaw, shoulders and hands.

• If your symptoms persist, repeat this technique for 3-5 minutes until you feel calm and relaxed.

There are also other ways to relax and Cope Stress

Go for a brisk walk. Never miss morning Renewals, has Meditation, Spend time in nature, petted

Sweat out tension with a good workout. Balance your diet to mostly alkaline food. Kindly avoid late dinner. Take an oil massage or bath periodically.

Laughing is considered the greatest stress let go.

Laugh without a reason. Those who laugh are healthy. Laughter is divinity and eternity.

Laughter should be unconditional.

Always allow your mind to have few minutes' peace because a peaceful mind can think well than a worked up Mind. Be radiant, ever smiling and ever loving.

Time is an asset, Handle it appropriately.

Time is money if and only that you manage it precisely and anticipate what to do with it. Everybody needs to acquire appropriate time management skills in order to be more productive. Controlling and dealing with your time legitimately permits you to spare some of it for self-improvement. One objective is to help yourself be mindful of how you utilize your time as one asset in sorting out, organizing, and prevailing in your work, with regards to contending exercises of companions, work, family, and so forth.

This is the motivation behind why a few officials complete their assignment sooner than others. Discipline is good in every aspect of life. Proper time management creates discipline, which makes you less likely to procrastinate.

Time Management disciplines that you create as a student can help you for rest of your life. Accomplish something today that your future will thank you for. It's critical to give yourself adequate time to deal with your studies in the event that you need to do well and you can spare yourself a considerable measure of stress when you manage your time well. Setting up a calendar for study, organizing your motivation with a careful time plan, separating your studies into smaller chunks and other time management abilities are a few of the basic methods. Track your objectives and arrange your groundwork.

Time Management has numerous privileged insights as indicated by everybody who judiciously utilized it. In spite of the fact that they may all look in an unexpected way, they can all be simplified into fundamentally privileged insights.

1.   Everybody's opportunity is limited, so ensure you get organized on the most vital agenda.

2.   Focus on what starts things out, utilize an ideal opportunity to do it proficiently.

3.   Prioritize on essential things. Segregate and classify and only do the activities that will directly or indirectly affect the outcome. Avoid other aspects. This might be the most critical key to time Management.

Regardless of the possibility that you outperform organizing the more imperative agenda, you ought to likewise figure out how to maximize the time when you work with them. In the event that you need to complete everything, you shouldn't squander valuable time particularly in the event that you just have a couple of it.

Multi-tasking might be a great accomplishment, however, consequences of multi-tasking may prompt to a low quality of work. You may have managed how to organize and how to allocate time for them. Be that as it may, you won't have the capacity to get done with anything in the event that you don't really work on them. Organizing and designating time are two important things needed to manage time.

On the off chance that the workload is more than what you can take in, you don't need to choose what to do complete first. You can chip away at each of them at little parts particularly in the event that they are all due on different deadlines. In this way, your fatigue and stress will be decreased on the grounds that this technique permits you to consider numerous things and thoughts as opposed to concentrating on one major work at once, which may prompt you to wear out. In the wake of completing the day's task, make another assignment list of all work you need to do on the next day.

A very famous illustration will throw more light on Time management implementation.

A teacher at a college is giving a pre-exam address on time management. Around his work area is a sack of sand, a pack of pebbles, some enormous stones, and pail. He requests a volunteer to put each of the three grades of stone into the pail, and a sharp student appropriately ventures up to complete the undertaking, beginning with the sand, then the rocks, then the stones, which don't all fit in the pail.

"This is a similarity of poor time management," trills the lecturer, "In the event that you'd have put the stones in, to begin with, then the pebbles, then the sand, each of the three would have fit. This is much similar to time administration, in that by finishing your greatest undertakings to start with, you leave space to finish your medium assignments, then your littler ones. By finishing your smallest task first, you invest such a great amount of energy in them you abandon yourself not able to finish either medium of substantial assignments palatably. Plan availabilities for your critical issues firs or the unavoidable, sand and water issues will top off your days and you won't fit the huge issues in.

I was in the Bank to get a draft, the work could have been the completed in 10-15 minutes time, however, took about an hour. The greatest intrusions in your workday every now and again originate from inside. Your colleagues represent an awesome risk to your viable time Management. What's doubly terrifying is that you don't generally perceive your associates as dangers. These people are in your group and they're the great folks, they're there for you! Nonetheless, it's imperative to perceive the indications of threat from time-squandering colleagues. If not, you're in danger of tumbling into the cordial fire. The present day workplace is regularly outlined on an open-office idea. Very few representatives are provided an office with an entryway, and generally, specialists are stooped in open work areas, frequently with allotments that do little to piece sets of collaborators. It should show a more brought together exertion and cooperation, I presume. Yet, it doesn't do much to ensure your freedom from your colleagues' interruptions on your time. If you encourage a colleague for 10 minutes, then a few colleagues will rob almost an hour of your productive time.

Postpone superfluous exercises until the work is finished!

Put off is the apogee of procrastinating. Delaying tasks or schedules that can be postponed until your school/office work is done! This can be the most difficult test of time management. As learners, we generally meet unexpected opportunities that look appealing, and then result in poor execution on a test, on a paper, or in preparing for an assignment. Diverting exercises will be more pleasant later without the pressure of the test, task, hanging over your head. Think as far as the pride of achievement. Rather than saying "no" figure out how to state "later".

There are challenges to Time Management

Everybody attempts genuine endeavours to get messages over to the family, companions, partners, business partners, and directors. Be that as it may, as these figures show, a number of those messages come up short since they're hazy, mistaken, or too long. Also, for each message that doesn't succeed, you squander time: rehashing, re-trying, revising, and rearranging. In this part, you find how to head off those issues by picking your medium and utilizing it adequately, keeping your message direct, and asking the right inquiries.

At the point when correspondence goes amiss, the effect is frequently unpretentious, however, no less tedious and costly. For example, in a study by a survey, representatives evaluated that more than 15% percent of their work week was squandered by poor correspondence.

Procrastinating is an effective propensity and many individuals are attracted to it. To conquer such mishap, there is an assortment of approaches to concentrate on your assignments without putting them off because of a considerable measure of reasons, The accompanying tips are helpful for beating tarrying to wind up more being more gainful in your work:

 Face your feelings of dread. Stalling may happen in view of Fear. Fear of what? You may have a lot of fears when you work. Fear of disappointment may make you delay and put off your tasks. You may be hesitant to commit errors, which is the reason you can't begin playing out your assignment. At times, there are individuals who fear to succeed. Keep in mind to dependably confront and overcome your apprehensions. This is a decent approach to crushing your procrastinating tendency.

When you start working on the tasks on your list. The tendencies of procrastination come into your mind particularly if there are diversions and allurements around you. At a specific time, you would end up considering "I'll simply do this later" or "regardless I have time tomorrow, I'll quite recently play for the present." If these musings come into your head, then this is an indication that you are going to put it off or linger. You need to perceive these signs and make an effort not to indulge into allurement. Rather, attempt to begin doing the assignment; you will then understand that the job needing to be done gets to be less demanding to do once you have begun on doing it.

A great many people discover procrastination is extremely troublesome, if not unthinkable, to stay away from. Be that as it may, in the event that you are totally mindful of the explanations behind procrastination, you'll know how to defeat it. Optimists are those who more easily shrug off their failures and multiply successes they are healthier, less stressed, and more successful. You can develop the traits of optimism and harness these benefits for yourself, and do better in your work culture.

Perseveringly take after your Plan

1) Your prosperity tomorrow relies on upon what moves you make today. Keep that in context so that the everyday choices you make are sufficiently keen.

2) Focus on the objectives you've set for yourself and follow up on your actual top needs.

3) Align your needs with your long haul qualities and objectives.

There are just 24 hours in a day. You might not have control over each booked hour of your day, however, you can control how effectively you utilize every moment, take after these tips on Time Management, and you will undoubtedly be fruitful in life.

****

Soft Skills for All- 2

1) Group Dynamics

2) Etiquettes

3) Anger Management

4) Motivation

5) Creativity and Innovation

6) Goal Setting

7) Counselling

8) Selling Skills

9) Presentation Skills

10) Public Speaking Skills

11) Risk Management

Group Dynamics Propel Enhanced Performance

We are all exceptionally acquainted with teams, however, the greater part of us are incredulous what a group is and how it is not at all like. Now and again it is hard to draw a refinement between a team and a group.

How can it vary? A team is by and large more particular, individuals required in a similar action with corresponding abilities that are focused on performing, specifically alluding to games and work, is a team. Colleagues cooperate toward a shared objective and share obligation regarding the team's prosperity. This arrangement is brief, short or seemingly perpetual and it differs in agreement.

The group is more than one individual that shares a typical character, goals and proceeding with cooperation. Say, a group of travellers going in a train has a typical component to travel, yet they are not really working towards a typical cause. Groups can be included of individuals of a similar race or social foundation.

Let us first observe with respect as to why individuals join a group. It is exceptionally obvious from the reality the individuals search for dependability and upgrades their accomplishment capacity. There are additionally different grounds which tempt individuals to join a group: To have a status, Security, Developing Self Esteem, Exercising Authority, Individual Goal accomplishment. In spite of the fact that the Management savants utilize these terms insightfully, this article would toss all the more light on Groups in Corporate and its Kinetics. As elucidated, teams can convey verbally, non-verbally and they are listed as formal and Informal.

The Formal Groups are an arrangement of individuals who meet up, constituted by the administration as a major aspect of the association structure. The essential part of formal teams is to advance the points and destinations of the association as set up in the plan and strategy articulation. This is done to satisfy needs or undertakings that are incorporated into its operation or hierarchical objectives. With a specific end goal to accomplish its definitive objective, an association makes sub-objectives which it allocates to various units or offices.

These formal groups made by the association itself are controlled by the authoritative guidelines and directions. The ideal group size is controlled by various components, as the quantity of individuals required to finish the assignment and the measure of coordination expected to cooperate. Bigger Groups are normally less powerful on the grounds that their individuals will devour additional time and exertion organizing their parts and settling their disparities.

The residency of the formal groups might be permanent or impermanent relying on the particular goals that have to be satisfied. Cases of permanent formal groups are the Board

Of Directors, overseeing boards of trustees and so on and transitory formal groups are exemplified by the team or impermanent panels made to satisfy certain predetermined destinations.

Informal groups are made deliberately and suddenly due to the socio-Psychological strengths working in the work environment. People cooperating frequently build up a liking for each other and they socialize with each other to beat their psychological fatigue, and dreariness related with their work. Informal groups are framed as they fulfill the social needs of people while at work. As they are not made by the association, the working of informal groups is not directed by hierarchical standards and controls. Informal groups are perpetually smaller in size. A person who is capacitated to tackle the burdens of different individuals turns into a Leader.

As indicated by Dr.Tuckman's hypothesis, there are five phases of group advancement: forming, storming, norming, performing, and adjourning. Amid these stages group, individuals must address a few issues and the path in which these issues are settled, this would figure out if the group will prevail with regards to fulfilling its assignments.

Forming: The initial stage marked with uncertainty and confusion. The structure is dubious. The administration can't be executed successfully. These sentiments reinforce in later phases of improvement. People are frequently befuddled amid this stage since roles are not clear and there may not be a solid leader.

Storming: There is a tremendous rift made due to different inconsistencies and contradiction among individuals. Individuals frequently challenge the group objectives and battle for power. People frequently eye for the administration position amid this phase of improvement. This is stage conflict surfaces and if individuals are not ready to resolve the conflict, then the group will frequently disband or battle to proceed yet will stay lethargic and never progress to alternate stages.

Norming; this is a stage when "I" is replaced by "We" This characterized by the recognition of individual differences and shared expectations. Expectantly, at this stage, the group members will begin to develop a feeling of group unity and identity. Cooperative effort should begin to yield results. Responsibilities are divided among members and the group decides how it will evaluate progress.

Performing: The group will begin acknowledging, they are very nearly achieving the objective. Cooperation shapes the very substance of the group. The doled out assignment is finished with devotion and assurance. This can happen when the group has now developed and accomplished sentiment cohesiveness. Amid this phase of advancement, people acknowledge each other and struggle is covered through intelligent group exchange. Individuals from the group settle on choices through a judicious procedure that is cantered on pertinent objectives instead of intense subject matters.

Adjourning. Not all groups encounter this phase of improvement since it is described by the disbandment of the group. A few groups are generally permanent and regrouping starts once more. A large portion of the individuals learn about so let and trouble immerses them as they get ready to take off.

Group has preferences and additionally drawbacks, augmentation from the perspective of individuals joining the group; there are likewise figures like upgrading efficiency. The individuals here are profited by working in a group and it encourages them to raise their yield. On the off chance that working in a group, everybody works durable utilizing their aptitudes to ensure quality yield. One more perspective is Information getting: While working in a group, everybody gets the chance to communicate to others inside the group. Every proposal is considered and deliberately examined before the group lands at a choice. Thus, we can find that the stream of discussion or correspondence is smooth and easy to the general population of the gathering. Choice taking individuals bring forth more prominent fulfilment. Look into recommends that dynamic individuals who are occupied with group critical thinking are more dedicated to the agreement and are enhanced happy with their support in the group than the individuals who were not included. There are different favourable circumstances likewise like Group Commitment, Methodology, Knowledge exchange, unwavering quality and so forth.

Talking about the burdens, an individual may command the examination. This prompts to individuals not sufficiently increasing fulfilment from the group since they feel excessively isolated in the basic leadership handle. A few individuals may depend too vigorously on others to take the necessary steps. This is a standout amongst the most noteworthy issues that groups confront. A few individuals don't contribute fittingly and help and don't sufficiently add to the gathering One answer for this issue is to make each gathering part mindful of the objectives and destinations of the group and in particular undertakings or obligations to every part. The rundown stretches out to natural clash, social loafing, subjective inclination, time limitations, and imagination misfortune and so on. One approach to assisting anticipates a conflict with individuals who avoid obligations is to keep the group small. It is hard to be a "loafer" or a "good-for-nothing" in a little group.

The group structure is an example of connections among individuals that hold the group together and help it accomplish relegated objectives. The structure can be depicted in various ways. Among the more common considerations are group size, group roles, group norms, and group cohesiveness.

Standards are the worthy benchmark of conduct inside a group that is shared by the individuals from the groups. Standards characterize the points of confinement of adequate and inadmissible conduct. They are normally made with a specific end goal to encourage bunch survival, make the conduct more unsurprising, abstain from humiliating circumstances, and express the estimations of the group. Each group will set up its own arrangement of standards that may decide anything from the fitting dress to what number of remarks, comments to make in a meeting. Groups apply pressure on individuals to drive them to fit in with the group's guidelines. The standards regularly mirror the level of duty, inspiration, and execution of the gathering. They are further named 1) Predictive-reason for comprehension 2) Relational-a few standards the conduct of others characterize connections 3) Control-direct the conduct of others.

Role Perception-An individual is relied upon to carry on as per his own particular observation in the group. Part Expectation-It is characterized as how others trust one ought to act in a given circumstance.

Cohesiveness alludes to the holding of group individuals and their yearning to remain some portion of the group. There are components impacting the measure of group cohesiveness. In General, it is viewed as more hard to get group enrolment the more strong the group. Cohesiveness in work group has numerous constructive outcomes, including labourer fulfilment, low turnover and non-attendance, and higher efficiency. Nonetheless, very durable groups might be negative to hierarchical execution if their objectives are skewed with authoritative objectives.

Give us a chance to take this story from the Mahabharata which assesses the viability of Group dynamics.Pandavas as a group could eclipse the Mighty Kauravas.Everyone revitalized behind Arjuna in Pandavas camp it was a well-weave strong gathering. While in Kauravas, however, Duryodhana was their Leader, the senior in their group were hesitant to battle the Pandavas. They were not a firm group.

The group progression in the Pandavas was well considered and in the case of any deviation in the gathering considering; Krishna won and dealt with things utilizing his emotional Intelligence. It was a task well cut out, one team one goal, to get back their lost kingdom.

There was no figure of emotional glue in Pandavas, Bheeshma, Dronacharya, and Kripacharya were educated researchers and they were in no state of mind to take any proclamation from their group Leader Dhuryodhana.Great Warrior Karna was battling his selective war of matchless quality with Arjuna.So everybody had their own agenda and the Kaurava group had no particular common goal. In spite of tremendous numbers, they lost the battle.

Evidence suggests that groups typically outperform individuals when the tasks involved require a variety of skills, experience, and decision-making. In Order to get the best of results, one needs to focus more on the benefits of working in a group. Thus, working together can be advantageous for the project, as well as the company.

****

Modern World Etiquettes

Modern World Etiquettes

A few people contend that etiquette does not make any difference anymore, that the principles of good conduct are out-dated and obsolete. In any case, great conduct and behaviour are never out of style. Etiquette, similar to all other social practices, advances, and coordinates with the times. Without behaviour, individuals from society would appear with an extreme degree of fretfulness and lack of regard for each other, which would prompt to put-down, untrustworthiness, road rage, fist fighting, and a rash of other disastrous episodes.

Etiquette is a code of amiable direct in light of social acknowledgment and effectiveness. Similarly, as there are traffic laws to make smooth transportation stream and anticipate crashes, so there are societal tenets intended to encourage positive human exchanges and decrease struggle. When you know the guidelines of etiquette for any given circumstance, it builds your solace, certainty, and skill, and by expansion, the simplicity and comfort of individuals around you. Today's etiquette plays a role in several important functions. Differentiating etiquette from manners; etiquette gives the frame or structure of which great manners work. Both are fundamental to viable human behaviour.

Etiquette gives individual security. Knowing how to carry on business properly in a given circumstance makes you more agreeable. It secures the sentiments of others. Appropriate manners require that you make others agreeable and secure their emotions. You don't bring up their blunders or attract attention to their missteps. It makes correspondence clearer. Manners upgrade correspondence by separating boundaries, not raising them. It will improve your status at work. In any working circumstance, you are seen as more skilled in the event that you know about the best possible set of principles for the working environment.

Whereas, exhibiting amateurish conduct could lose your business. Here are essential manners' rules you ought to be following. As times are changing, so do social standards for individual and expert conduct, yet that doesn't mean fundamental behaviour doesn't make a difference.

Execution and quality are vital, as well, obviously, yet not only. We now and again overlook that business is about individuals. There is no deficiency of equipped and dependable individuals in the business world and behaviour can have the effect. Wouldn't you rather team up with, work for or purchase from somebody who has elevated expectations of expert conduct? Numerous, however not all take after these 10 time-tried tenets of better conduct.

A handshake is still the expert standard. Not just does this basic motion show that you're well mannered, sure and receptive, it likewise sets the tone for any potential future expert relationship. In an exceptionally easygoing work air, you may have the capacity to escape with a gesture or a welcome, however, it's justified, despite all the trouble to attempt to offer your hand.

The first person who reaches the door holds it for the next person regardless of the gender. Keeping fingers together with an open palm while pointing is advised. Pointing the index finger alone is aggressive.

Say "Please" and "Thank you" a few times amid the discussion, or else it will weaken the effect and may perhaps make you weak and needy. This ought to abandon saying, yet even in an exceptionally easygoing expert air, this fundamental type of obligingness is still objective. Saying "Excuse me, I am sorry" will never bring you down. Today, sending a thank you email is splendidly adequate, yet a written by hand card to say thanks is dependably a pleasant touch.

 Try not to interfere. We've turned into a country of "over-talkers," so anxious to offer our own particular conclusions or press our point that we frequently intrude on others mid-sentence. It can be tongue-bitingly hard to constrain ourselves not to add, particularly when the discourse is warmed. Don't. It's impolite and shows affront for the feelings of others. Keep in mind, be emphatic, not forceful.

Watch your dialect. Verbal and composed correspondences are frequently considerably less formal than in times past, yet be mindful so as to pick your words astutely. Obviously, a harsh, impolite or hostile dialect is unsuitable, however so is slang. While it might be ordinary to our general public, it's never adequate in an expert air.

Try not to talk. It's so difficult some of the time to oppose taking part in somewhat "safe" chatter. Be that as it may, actually babble is never innocuous. It is unquestionably harming to the subject of the chatter, yet it likewise thinks about inadequately you. It's regular to be interested and inspired by what other individuals are doing, yet discussing somebody who is not present is impolite. Try not to listen stealthily. Everybody is qualified for private discussions, face to face or via telephone. The same goes for email; don't remain behind someone and read their messages.

Recognize others. When somebody approaches you, recognize him or her. In case you're really busy something vital, its fine to request that they hold up a moment while you wrap up. In the event that you pass somebody in the passage or in the city, yet don't have sufficient energy to talk, in any event, wave a hand and make proper acquaintance. Hecticness is not a reason to disregard individuals.

Be on time. We're all occupied. Being prompt shows others that you esteem their time. Being late doesn't imply that you're busier than other individuals; it just implies that you're rude. No telephone amid gatherings. When you're in a meeting, concentrate on the meeting examination. Try not to accept calls, content or check email. It's impolite to alternate participants, also, greatly irritating. It likewise makes gatherings last longer on the grounds that the members continue losing centre.

Communication etiquette

It's at times not what you say, but instead how you say it that matters! Kindly return phone calls and email within 24 hours - paying little mind to the likelihood that solitary to say that you will give requested information at a later date. Dismissing a mobile call is considered extremely harsh, you can, on the other hand, turn off your volume with the goal that you can give back the call later. Never send a forward message to a customer, regardless of the possibility that the matter is same ensure each is sent exclusively.

Ask before putting somebody on speakerphone.

Customize your voice message - there's nothing more regrettable than simply listening to a telephone number on somebody's voice message and not knowing whether you are leaving a message with the right individual. Individuals may not leave messages.

A standout amongst the most generally disregarded tenets of etiquette today is that every individual merit the touch of peace and quiet. The individual sitting alongside you or opposite you wouldn't like to be a persuasively held prisoner to whatever sounds you might listen to or make. Remember these decorum tips with a specific end goal to regard other's "sound space."

Comprehend messaging, do not spam or simply forward a message which you are receiving. Confine yourself sending great and viable messages only. Do not forward gossips, unauthorized promulgation.

Messages at work ought to be linguistically right and free of spelling mistakes. They ought not to be dealt with like individual email. Whenever messaging, utilize the subject box, and ensure it specifically identifies with what you are composing. Sending a message in capital letters is "shouting". These guarantees ease in thinking that it's later and a possibly speedier reaction. Never say in an email anything you wouldn't say to somebody's face. Underlining, emphasizing, bolding, shading, and changing text dimension can make a gentle email message appear to be excessively solid or forceful.

Especially for Men

Run private with your disturbing propensities. This is somewhat unique, yet in the event that there is something that you do that is greatly irritating to the next individuals throughout your life, such as spitting on the street, burping after a feast, smoking cigarettes, scratching private parts, chewing a paan. Bathe your body and brush your teeth consistently. Cut the fingernails and toenails. Look for the errant nose and ear hairs. Take a look at yourself in the mirror at least once per day, notice yourself, and apply an endorsed antiperspirant. Ensure you put on clean socks;

innerwear and clothing. Never wear t-shirt or jeans on a weekday to the office. Long sleeve shirts should always be buttoned at the cuff but should never be rolled up.

Never permit your hair to hang down on your neck. Hair ought to be perfect flawlessly trimmed and arranged. Never leave home without shaving. On the off chance that you are wearing a moustache don't worry about it, ensure it is trimmed properly. Wash your hands. It is stunning that there are men and ladies, too who don't wash their hands in the wake of utilizing the restroom or before sitting to eat. Make somewhat sure to clean with a piece of scrub.

Make sure you stand when shaking someone's hand. Never check WhatsApp, messages, or Instagram when eating with someone. Don't give an assessment of a book or motion picture unless you've seen or perused it. Whether you're driving with a visitor or in the front seat, never remain on the telephone for longer than a moment. It's discourteous to the next individual who can't listen to music and needs to hear one portion of a discussion.

An etiquette guide can't address each conceivable circumstance you will confront as you travel through life. There are innumerable circumstances in life when you will have the chance to practice little kindnesses that will uncover your actual character. Every little demonstration may enhance another person's life a bit and that individual may pass it on to another person, so set aside the opportunity to show graciousness to outsiders.

On the off chance that each of us practices both the little and expansive motions of etiquette consistently to everyone around us that we scarcely know, the impact will rapidly spread, making life much more pleasant for everyone of us.

****

Managing Anger.

Let us first know, it is the secondary emotion which cause's anger, fear is the chief essential source of all anger. If you've problems coping with your anger, fright is most possibly the supply of your trouble. Whilst you discover the way to cope with fearfulness you're taking a big soar in the direction of commanding your lifestyles. Making use of rational self-speaks strategies is considered the best key for addressing worry. If negative questioning is a part of your each day life, you are able to effortlessly adjust your state of mind by abiding few guidelines.

Outrage can be typical and solid feeling that helps us instinctually identify and react to an undermining circumstance. More than this, when it is appropriately directed, it can be an intense propelling power; we as a whole know how hard we can function to cure an undeniable treachery.

Nonetheless, it can likewise be a feeling that gains out of power, prompting to stress, trouble, awfulness, and despondency. Uncontrolled rage can genuinely hurt your own and expert life since it can turn out to be unimaginably damaging to yourself and the general people around you.

Like other emotions, anger brings in physiological and biological changes; while you get angry, your coronary artery contracts more and blood strain goes up, as do the stages of your power hormones, adrenaline, and noradrenalin. Anger may be as a result of each external and internal activity. You could be indignant at a selected individual, which include a colleague or manager or an event, a traffic jam, a cancelled flight, or your anger might be due to stressful or brooding approximately your non-public issues. Reminiscences of traumatic or enraging occasions also can trigger angry emotions.

Every person feels anger at different times, to various tiers. It's simply a part of the human enjoy. Feelings of anger can get up in many ones of kind contexts. Experiencing unjust treatment; hearing a criticism, or really now not getting what you need are but most of the capacity triggers. The enjoy of anger can range from slight infection to frustration, the entire manner up with seething rage. As a count of truth, even boredom is a slight version of anger in the form of dissatisfaction with what is occurring. Folks that are easily angered typically have a low tolerance for frustration. They cannot take matters in stride, and they're particularly infuriated if the state of affairs seems one way or the other unjust: as an instance, being corrected for a minor mistake. The intention of anger control is to reduce both your emotional, emotions and the physiological arousal that triggers reasons. You cannot eliminate, or keep away from, the materials or the humans that enrage you, nor can you exchange them, however, you could learn to manipulate your reactions.

In step with Jerry Deffenbacher, Ph.D., a psychologist who specializes in anger control, some humans actually are more "hot-headed" than others are; they get indignant more without problems and more intensely than the common man or woman does. There also are people who do not display their anger in loud amazing methods, however, are chronically irritable and grumpy. Easily angered people don't continually curse and throw matters; sometimes they withdraw socially, sulk, or get bodily sick.

When you're feeling anger, whether mild or strong, hold for a moment to check in with yourself and notice if you could pick out the primary emotion driving the anger. If it's that difficult to name it, but the anger, start exploring your mind, as to what fuel feelings. Try to understand the swing from a primary emotion like anxiety, worry or unhappiness into anger mode. It is quite common and fast, and it is at the subconscious level. Feeling anger can create a dependency for you, this tantamount to taking more time to fish out the skunked thoughts and feelings that lie low on memory. A negative response can harm relationships and cause a loss of respect and self-appreciate. This is particularly the case whilst we react right away and angrily to what we perceive to be a threat, however, where that belief is inaccurate. This may go away, making us look very foolish.

A man asked a monk, "How can anger be subdued?" The monk asked, "How do you subdue a fire?" the person answered, "through the water." "In addition, anger may be subdued with the aid of final calm," stated the monk. "When a person incites and provokes me, then how can I no longer get irritated and remain calm?" wondered the man. The monk asked, "Do you go to your spouse house with your children?" "Sure," answered the person. "Do they offer you lunch and comfort you in their residence to stay?" asked the monk. "Sure," replied the man. "However if their offer isn't appealing to you, then what takes place to their food and safe haven?" asked the monk. "They remain with them," answered the person. The monk explained, "in addition, if you do no longer accept anger, then regardless of how absolutely everyone provokes you to become indignant, the anger stays with the alternative man or woman. Having no anger, you will no longer get angry and could remain calm."

Anger and Ego go together. Ego is part of your mind that believes the entirety turns around yourself. Every person lives in his own world and is expecting the whole thing must move the way he thinks, is excellent. Your regulation is the right one and people of others are questionable and perhaps even incorrect. We do now not truly concentrate on others, due to the fact after they speak, we have already got our very own tale standby and we are able to hardly ever wait to inform it. The purpose is that we need to pressure our factor of view on others. An ego is a place in a human body, which is there because humans consider that most effective one aspect is crucial: I need to survive! Whatever it takes, I should live to tell the tale.

Manage Anger Now!!!

Know while you're angry, there are often both physical and emotional signs of anger and, by way of recognizing these, we're more likely so as to manipulate them. Viable physical signs and symptoms of Anger, You rub your face often. Tightly clasping one hand with the alternative, or making clenched fists, clenching of the jaw, grinding teeth or bruxism. By experiencing Shallow breathing and/or breathlessness. Increased heart-rate and perspiring, sweaty arms it is considered a symptom of anger. Trembling or shaking lips, arms, rocking movement, even as sitting. You come to be impolite and lose your feel of humour. You speak louder. You broaden cravings for matters which you assume may additionally relax you: tobacco, sugar, alcohol, capsules, consolation meals, and so on, as feasible emotional symptoms of Anger. Anger causes a desire to 'run away' from the scenario, feeling sad or depressed, feeling guilty or resentful. Tension, feeling disturbing can appear in lots of one of the kind methods. A feeling or desire to lash out verbally or physically.

Assume before you talk, regularly we have a tendency to say vicious things in the heat of the moment, in the bargain, we both get into more problem and remorse our actions. Suppose what you need to think whether you should in any respect say it or simply randomly blurting out.

Blow steam at the SPA, Working out is a brilliant manner to release pent-up frustration and stress. When you indulge in some energetic bodily hobby, glad hormones, including serotonin and endorphin are launched inside the body. Other blessings consist of an in shape frame and higher health. Take a recess, Are you recognized for having an uncongenial temper? It is exceptional if you do not plunge into a heated dialogue. Of path, that does not imply you endure it.

Take a small break, go out for a quick walk, drink some water, wash your face and then, as the conflicting person and you have cooled down, cross ahead and make your factor. Sleep properly, Sleep deprivation can lead us to emerge as cranky, irritable, have mood swings, negative concentration and occasional tolerance for a strain. So, if you have not been getting sufficient sleep for a while now, it's time to adjust your day by day agenda, such that you may get a great eight hours of sleep.

Cheer up, occasionally, even after we've indulged in a verbal duel, we generally tend to brood over the scenario. And this ruins the rest of the day. To keep away from this, divert your mind and cheer up, concentrate on your preferred song, watch funny videos or study jokes on the internet, play games on your computer or your cell phone. Even ingesting something excellent would possibly raise your mood.

Guidance rest strategies, Meditation, and yoga are noticeably advocated those with anger-control issues. If these aren't your aspect, trying to write a diary/journal. Remind yourself that getting irritated is not going to mend something, that it may not make you feel better, logic defeats anger, because anger, even when it is justified, can hasten to end up irrational. So use bloodless hard logic on yourself.

Remind yourself that the world is "not out to get you," you're just experiencing some of the hard spots of the day by day existence, do this whenever you sense anger getting the exception of you, and it will help you get a more balanced perspective. Irritated humans have a tendency to call for things that have fairness, appreciation, settlement, willingness. If anyone desires these are all hurt and disillusioned while we do not get them, but irritated human demand them, and whilst their needs are not met, their disappointment becomes angry. As part of their cognitive restructuring, indignant people need to be aware of their annoying nature and translate their expectations into goals.

It's natural to get defensive when you're criticized, however, don't fight returned. Alternatively, concentrate to what is underlying the words: the message that this character might feel disregarded and unloved. It can take a whole lot of patient thinking of your element, and it can require some respiratory space, but do not allow your anger or a partner', let a discussion spin out to manipulate, by keeping cool, can preserve the state of affairs from turning into a disastrous one.

****

Stay Motivated...

What stimulates you? What fires you up? With what are you energetic and excited about? What do you do to get encouraged? All you need is boosting your psyche. Motivation is about mental and human perspective. It is the way towards nurturing ability among the representatives to do work in an ideal way. It is the demonstration of inspiring workers to accomplish hierarchical destinations. Motivation is to a great degree individual and specific to each and every person. What influences me is my passion, say even to your love, she gets propelled going to place of worship.

Motivation is an intricate and complicated task. Human needs are boundless and they are variable as indicated by time and circumstance. A fulfilled individual of the present may not be fulfilled later on. In a comparative way, even same people may not be inspired by comparable behaviour and workplace. Subsequently, an administrator must be more cognizant to inspire his staffs and to accomplish targets.

Often, people cast off the chances of a lively employee with persuading agents. They may be associated, yet motivation truly portrays the level of longing for specialists feels to perform, paying little notice to the level of fulfillment. It is their business to spur delegates to do their occupations well. So how do chiefs do this? The answer is motivation in the organization, the technique through which supervisors ask laborers to be productive and feasible. Certain individuals have found an adequate harmony between their commitment to others and their own particular desires and needs. This helps them to feel fulfilled and to remain positive. We see this about them at work and socially in light of the fact that it's reflected in their behaviour, their way to deal with life and the way they perform.

Imparting motivation isn't simple, yet it's important on the off chance that you need your workers to develop and remain happy with their occupations. It's the driving force that leads individuals to work harder, which means more efficiency for your company and the most vital contributing element to in general fulfilment, which prompts to higher employee retention. That being said, there isn't any single methodology that can mystically spur every one of your workers without a moment's delay and keep them inspired all through their business. Everybody is different, with interesting qualities and thoughts, and in the event that you need to be fruitful in imparting inspiration to everyone, you need to discover various methodologies to contact every person.

Here a leader plays a crucial role.

As a leader in an Organisation, individuals will look to you to set an example for whatever remains of the crowd. Will set a tone for them to follow, a hard working attitude, and preparation of qualities for the organization whether you intend to do directly or not, and setting the correct case can meaningfully affect the mindset of your gathering. For instance, in the event that you are positive and remain hopeful about everything, even notwithstanding huge difficulties, your staffs will be probably going to do model you. In the event that you set a case of energy and comprehension, your professionals will reflect you, and the whole culture of the workplace will turn out to be all the more encouraged. In a bigger organization, it's vital to pass on this idea to every one of the leaders who work independently with others, particularly managers and bosses. Having reliable great cases no matter how you look at it can significantly change the scene of your working environment.

Interpersonal relations, most likely, shape the key of workplace Motivation. When we discuss interpersonal relations, it is from the CEO to subordinate staff in the workplace. Numerous companies consistently train their workers formally by professional trainers so that entomb individual relations are very much kept up and projected objectives are accomplished. One ought to note that great relationships do not mean bargain in work. The relationship can be well maintained from the executive level to Supervisor with decisiveness in work territory yet at the same time propel their groups by setting up the affinity with every last individual from the group and supporting them on their individual issues.

Most employees need a bit of motivation to like their occupations and perform ideally. A few employees may be craving for cash while others discover acknowledgment and rewards expressly inspiring.

Incentives

An incentive is a rousing impact that is intended to drive conduct and propel employees to deliver quality work. The employers utilize various types of motivations to increase production. Employee's incentives arrive in a variety of forms including paid time off, rewards, and money and travel advantages. These motivators drive employees inspiration since they offer workers more to make progress toward the target than a regular salary check. This old fable can be a vibrant example for employees on motivation

There was an old donkey. One day coincidentally he fell into the rancher's well. The rancher has assessed the circumstance and contemplated internally, that neither the well nor the old donkey was justified regardless of the endeavours to spare them. He decided and chose to cover the old donkey with earth in the well. Therefore, the neighbours assembled and they began to scoop soil into the well. The old donkey was panicked and insane in the first place. Yet, soon one cheerful thought struck a chord – each time when a scoop of soil arrived on his back, he would shake it off and venture up!

He rehashed these words to himself and once more: „Shake it off and venture up". Along these lines, he could battle the frenzy and empower himself. After some time, the donkey had ventured over the well's divider. Although he was totally drained, he was the victor, he spared his own particular life. He chose to face his difficulty emphatically and not to surrender, and in this manner, he won. What seemed to bury him actually saved him, owing to his confidence and relentless efforts? Employees taking a cue out of this should follow the same when there are any negative remarks, bullying or provoke in workplace.

Maslow motivational hypothesis suggests

☐　　　Physiological needs, food, water, shelter, sleep etc.We can move up the hierarchy once this need is met.

☐　　　Safety; secured safety or to an extent financial safety much needs to function efficiently.

☐　　　Love and belonging: this comes next when the above two needs are met.

❑   Esteem comes when these needs are achieved, the level of self-worthiness that others are very much aware of his competence and value.

❑   To achieve the above 4 tasks are not that easy, the person is ready to strive for highest level self-actualisation. That is a state of self-fulfillment, where people realize their highest potential.

Cognitive Evaluation Theory has two dimensions the intrinsic and extrinsic motivators.

This hypothesis proposes that there are really two inspiration frameworks: inborn and extraneous that compare to two sorts of motivators: natural motivators: Achievement, obligation, and ability. The workforce that originates from the real execution of the assignment or occupation is the characteristic enthusiasm of the work.

Extrinsic: Results, refinement, input, environment - things that originate from a man's domain, controlled by others. Either of these might be an even more capable motivator for a given person. Naturally, inspired people to perform their own particular accomplishment and fulfillment. On the off chance that they come to a belief that they are doing some work as a result of the compensation or the working conditions or some other outward reason, they start to lose inspiration.

According to Kevin Lee pages' the origin of motivation: It's in your head". The all-important neurotransmitter dopamine has a great role to play. Investigations of dopamine started with delight until specialists started seeing exceptional wonders. They saw spikes in dopamine amid snapshots of high anxiety. Dopamine ascended on account of fighters with PTSD who heard gunfire. Stress and gunfire are not pleasurable marvels, yet their dopamine was high. Plainly dopamine went past unimportant pleasure, and it turns out dopamine's actual impact might be an inspiration. Dopamine plays out it's undertaking before we get rewards, implying that its genuine occupation is to urge us to act and inspire us to accomplish or abstain from something terrible.

Tips to stay Motivated;

Accomplishing objectives is not a matter of having "discipline".

It's a matter of rousing yourself and keeping your emphasis on your objective.

Post a photo of your objective somewhere noticeable.

Envision your objective unmistakably, every day, for no less than 5-10 minute.

Break it into littler, smaller than normal objectives.

Discover Inspiration to remain propelled to accomplish long haul objective.

Give it time, be tolerant.

****

Creativity & Innovation

"Creativity is connecting things. When you ask creative people how they did something, they feel a little guilty because they didn't really do it, they just saw something. It seemed obvious to them after a while. That's because they were able to connect experiences they have had and synthesize new things." - Steve Jobs, Founder of Apple Inc.

Creativity and innovation address the methods for improving in an unpredicted way. Creativity is a thought creation. Somebody being creative is thinking of new thoughts. How do Creativity and Innovation vary is the substance of this article. Creative thoughts are new and fitting. The fittingness of the thought is basic as these creative thoughts require quality and in addition inventiveness.

Creativity is the demonstration of transforming new and inventive thoughts into reality. Here new creative depiction is described by the capacity to see the world in a new dimension, to discover concealed parameters, to make associations between apparently irrelevant surprises, and to create a clear solution. It can be termed that creativity includes two procedures: cognition, then delivering. In the event that you have thoughts, however, if you don't follow up on them, you are considered imaginative but far from creative. Creativity is action.

Creativity starts with an establishment of information, taking a fresh discipline, and acting to a state of mind. You figure out how to be novel by testing, investigating, addressing presumptions, utilizing creative energy and blending data. Figuring out how to be creative is likened to playing and learning a game. It requires practice to build up the correct technique and a strong situation in which to thrive.

Clayton M. Christensen and his researchers uncovered, "that your capacity to create imaginative thoughts is not simply an element of the awareness, but rather additionally a component of five key practices that advance your brain for disclosure." Partnering: illustrating the associations between inquiries, issues, or thoughts from random fields.

Addressing: posturing inquiries that test basic intelligence. Watching: examining the conduct of clients, providers, and contenders to distinguish better approaches for getting things done.

Organizing: meeting individuals with various thoughts and points of view. Testing: Building intuitive encounters and inciting irregular reactions to seeing what bits of knowledge rise.

In the early 50's creativity was frequently thought to be a capacity had just by the talented few; in the 60s it was regularly connected with abilities of mental adaptability that could be learned. In the 70s the part of the significant experience was all the more completely valued by analysts, and in the 80s, attention was attracted to the key part of natural creativity. These speculations concentrate on inattentiveness at the level of the individual; all the more as of late directors and specialists have turned their regard for the part played by the social setting. In the 90s associations gave careful consideration such that works culture and this society and the environment has the potential for imagination on individuals in associations. In the present thousand years, the concentration has moved towards understanding inventiveness as a developing wonder that expands on what has gone before and emerges from progressing connections, a point of view that considers the part social setting plays in the beginning of thoughts. We will consider the ramifications of these hypotheses.

One school of thought links Creativity to Change, they draw induction referring to both are two sides of a coin. Inventive pioneers welcome development, urge others to drop obsolete methodologies and go out on a risk. To build up a feeling of possession among workers, it is important to include representatives in basic leadership. The authority of the top administration lifts subordinate's vision to higher sights. The Creative Leader is focused on a procedure of ceaseless change and is skilful in managing change. They comprehend the contrast amongst static and imaginative associations and try to make their association creative.

Even today In CISCO, every six months, they have 'best practices' meetings where staff from various locations meet and discuss the best practices of their offices located all over the country. By leveraging the strengths of their employees' creativity and by creating a common forum for the exchange of ideas.

Creative people may be challenging for the manager. They are serious about their work, and even the process of reviewing performance evaluations may be difficult because it is hard to measure creative accomplishment. Creative people tend to have diverse intellectual and personality characteristics from their less creative equivalents. In general, Creative people are more psychologically flexible than others which allow them to overcome the conventional ways of looking at problems. Creative workers tend to be bright rather than brilliant. Extraordinary high intelligence is not required to be creative but creative people are good at generating options.

A more modern point of view concentrates less on who is and is not inventive and more on various styles of innovativeness. Kirton proposes there is a case for separating between the "inventive" way to deal with imagination, which includes reframing issues and concocting drastically new methodologies, and the "versatile" approach, which includes enhancing existing practice incrementally. He recommends there is a continuum crosswise over individuals supporting an inventive approach, including doing things any other way, to wanting to improve. In Western social orders, we tend to partner creativity with imaginative leaps forward, however, most developments occur through a progression of incremental upgrades. Up to this point, the versatile style of innovativeness is expanding on what has gone before and it has gotten less consideration in the West yet has apparently been exceptional refreshing in the East.

Innovation can be named Radical and Incremental. Michael Kirton separates between trailblazers, who do things any other way, and adaptors, who improve. There are events when an individual or group can propose a radical in a better approach for doing things that seem to owe little to be tried and the true way of thinking or past practice. Such spasmodic change may reasonably be viewed as 'Risky'. Should it require significant venture to get it going, many hazards loath administration groups may take a lot of persuading before support such an attempt.

The principle contrast between creativity and Innovation is the focus or the core interest. Creativity is about unleashing the capability of the cognition to consider new thoughts. Those ideas could show themselves in any number of ways, however regularly, they get to be something we can see, listen, notice, touch, or taste. Nonetheless, innovative thoughts can likewise be thought explores inside one individual's psyche.

Creativity is subjective, making it difficult to gauge. Innovation is the implementation of something new. Creativity is Imaginative whereas innovation is Productive. Thinking something new is Creativity, developing and application of new ideas is Innovation.

Innovation, then again, is totally quantifiable. Innovation is about bringing change into moderately stable frameworks. It's additionally concerned about the work required to make a thought reasonable. By recognizing an unrecognized and neglected need, an association can utilize development to apply its imaginative assets to outline a proper arrangement and to reap the best ROI.

Organizations which are genuine about fostering advancement need to grapple with two primary issues: Risk taking and disappointment repugnance. All innovations include risk, and all dangers incorporate the likelihood of disappointment. Disappointment ought to never be viewed as a blot; it is a learning background. Leaders and their Organisation can't fear of failure. Obviously, the very term "innovation" suggests something new and diverse. As yet, focusing on organizations that are reliably inventive in their ventures. Consider these organizations that the utilization of design thinking to accomplish their key objectives:

According to statistics available "India has changed in this decade from being a nonspecific innovation administration provider to an advanced driver of worldwide free market activity for innovation. India today remains on the edge of the following rush of development with accentuation on innovation and computerized change to be the key empowering agents".

This illustration demonstrates the glaring difference; the creation of the bike was the greatest innovation over scooters. In 1960, individuals used to go on scooters, for which they need to kick the starter from the side for it to fire up. Along these lines, a long time passed, and no one even thought for the innovation. The innovation of the motorbike made them understand that they can likewise ride bikes without endeavouring any additional endeavours, they simply need to tap the switch and its begins consequently. In this example, the thought of motorcycle is creativity, but the real invention or putting it to use is innovation.

There is unvaryingly a question between creativity and Innovation as both are critical for an Organisation to last more. The presence of both can prompt to achievement. After broaching on this extensively, we should think about how to be creative, by making inquiries, reaching inferences, testing and investigating new thoughts and augmenting the regions of considering. For being innovative, we must be able to take the risk, testing, making inquiries and watching things. Fear of failure should be brushed aside.

****

Goal Setting

Setting goals in some cases is intense, though the harder step is choosing the correct goal. Goal setting is an essential strategy for settling on what is expected to accomplish in your life, by separating it into vital and unimportant parts. It will help you endlessly pursue with fearlessness, the effective accomplishment of said goals. One can pick a goal that you feel important for your wellbeing, strength, and happiness. There are many advantages in setting goals. Setting goals can leverage in achieving, improving more in a lifetime. It also boosts the self-confidence of an individual. Personal planning can also be termed as goal setting. To achieve better results, it is best advised to set goals on a routine basis. Goals are set to be achieved.

 It is initiated by breaking them into smaller and reachable targets. Essential planning is a criterion where you can start working on it. Once you have set a long term goal to say spanning 20 years, it can be divided into smaller goals of 4 years where it can be accomplished. These 4 years need to be sub-divided in one year, six months and even 1 month in order to achieve the long-term perspective.

Making S.M.A.R.T. Goals

Make them "keen." This is an acronym, as you presumably know, and it is deciphered in different courses by various instructors. When I allude to Smart Goals, I mean this. Objectives must meet five criteria. They should be Specific, Measurable, Attainable, Realistic and Time-bound.

Specific—your objectives must distinguish precisely what you need to achieve in as much specificity as you can gather.

Need to study more is a vague goal.

Need to study more on Soft Skills is a Specific Goal.

Quantifiable: as the familiar saying says, "you can't oversee what you can't gauge." If conceivable, attempt to measure the outcome. You need to know completely, decidedly regardless of whether you hit the objective.

Need to acquire more money this year-Vague

Need to acquire Rs 50,000 more this year is quantifiable.

Attainable: each objective ought, to begin with, an activity and achievable.

Consistently compose articles each week; tall objective

Composing 2 decent articles this week-Is attainable and feasible.

Realistic—one must be cautious here. A decent objective ought to extend you; however, you need to include a measurement of judgment skills. I go up to the edge of my usual range of familiarity and afterwards venture over it.

Science understudy trying to end up distinctly as a Chartered Accountant-Unrealistic-Some would have succeeded, however, many have fizzled.

A science understudy can seek to end up distinctly as a Doctor is Realistic.

Time-bound—each objective needs a date connected with it. At the point when do you plan to convey on that objective? It could be by year-end or it could be a more close term. An objective without a date is only a fantasy. Ensure that each objective closures with a by when date.

Need to get fit No time determined.

Need to get more fit by Dec 31-Time bound.

Write and review periodically. This is essential. There is enormous power in recording your goals regardless of the possibility that you never build up an activity, arrange or do whatever else. When you write something down, you are expressing your goal and getting things under way. Writing your goals is a cognitive practice in itself; the genuine justice is in checking on them all the time.

The act of goal setting is not simply supportive; it is a prerequisite for happiness. Psychologists opine that individuals who gain steady ground toward important goals live more joyful more fulfilled lives than the individuals who don't. In the event that you don't have schedule goals, let me encourage you to make a booked time on your schedule to chip away at it. You can complete a portrayal in as meagre as an hour or two. Certain things pay rich dividends for such a docile speculation.

In the working environment, goal setting keeps representatives spurred and centred and help the operation run all the more productively. Goals can go from expert development to monetary benefits and ought to give a dream and reason to all included. Working environment goals ought to be sensible, concentrate on making enhancements.

Express your goal in a positive way. This is a fundamental factor for you to attain the objective. If you are less confidence on the goal you have set there is every possibility of the goal going skewed. There is nothing more disturbing than failing to achieve a personal goal for reasons that are beyond your control. That situation sucks. There are two types of goals learning goals and performance goals. 1.) Learning goals: Tasks where skills and knowledge can be acquired 2.) Performance goals, selecting tasks that are easily achievable.

Organisational Goals

Organisational objectives are those intended to enhance the structure of a business and organisation completely. It is useful to separate vast hierarchical objectives into littler ones to make them seem less scary. For instance, a goal can integrate and can be attractive to the Organisation. Its improvement inside an organisation by intensifying representative trust and inspiration, the sharing of organisation objectives, making a culture of support and empowering worker development. Since Organisational improvements are a substantial objective, break down the due dates into quick goals, transient goals and long haul goals, and incorporate activity ventures, and in addition approaches to gauge the achievement of each.

Employee Goals

To help employees have a feeling of motivation in an organisation and feel propelled, it is critical for everyone to have individual, proficient goals. It is basic for workers to set up individual goal amid a yearly review, yet the creation and ongoing review and new objectives can expand employee's prosperity. The employee goal can be acquiring a promotion, increasing more responsibilities, going about as a Project head, increasing more customers for the organisation or bagging an organisation reward. At the point when an employee makes a goal, his manager can demonstrate his support by encouraging him to create activity steps, making due dates flexible and lavishly praising even a small triumph.

Financial Goals

It is normal for work environment goals to incorporate those identified with accounts. While making short-and-long term money related goals, it is essential to tell employees about the vision and make courses for every individual to take part. By conveying the significance of a monetary objective and how the organisation will utilise the cash, employees will probably make the organisation's money related goals an individual objective. Make the action steps related to financial objectives ones that use and enhance employee talents and creativity.

"In the late 1960s, Edwin Locke proposed that intentions to work toward a goal are a major source of work motivation. That is, goals tell an employee what needs to be done and how much effort will need to be expended. The evidence strongly supports the value of goods. More to the point we can say that specific goal increase performance; that difficult goal, when accepted result in higher performance than do easy goals; and that feedback leads to higher performance than does non-feedback. Specific goals produce a higher level of output than does the generalised goal of 'do you best'. Why? The specificity of the goal itself seems to act as an internal stimulus".

Why some face failure in Goal setting.

As we saw before not to set unrealistic goals is not specifically reverse by setting goals that are low. One has a tendency to do this on fear of disappointment and they basically linger. So set an objective which is over the immediate grasp. Numerous people refrain from setting objectives since they endeavoured it once and when they didn't fulfil them, they picked goal setting basically doesn't work. The reason goal setting misses the mark is by virtue of the objective setter has not taken after the means important to build up clear, engaged objectives that make a guide for achievement.

There are grey areas where goal setting goes wrong, Setting excessively numerous goals when you begin setting goals, you may see numerous things that you need to fulfil. So you begin setting goals in all ranges. The issue with this is you have a settled sum time and vitality. In the event that you attempt to concentrate on various goals without a moment's delay, you can't give singular goals the consideration they merit.

Rather, utilise the "quality" and not amount" manage when setting goals. Work out the relative significance of everything that you need to finish throughout the following six to twelve months. At that point pick close to, say, three goals to concentrate on. Keep in mind, the achievement of your work towards an objective lays on concentrating on only a couple of things at once. On the contrary that you constrain the quantity of goals you're chipping away at, you'll adequate time and energy to schedule and do things truly well!

All through each individual's life, a person may have one or many goals that they set for themselves. There are different varieties of goals. Whether they are short term, long haul or simply impermanent, the essential thing is that we remain steady, centred and keeps our eyes on the goal. There are times while achieving a goal might be simple or different circumstances when it appears like a goal is far away and we will never have the capacity to achieve it is yet in the event that we don't lose heart and continue not to buckle down, a goal can be accomplished.

Goal setting is an intense procedure for considering your optimal future, and for motivating yourself to transform your vision of this future into reality. The way toward setting goals helps you pick where you need to go in life.

****

Presentation Skills

Presenting clear information which can be easily conjugated by all the intended recipients is a handy skill to possess. Today, presentation skills are required in practically every field. Presentations are the best, and frequently the only chance you have to impact the decision makers. For an effective presentation, one ought to be an effective speaker. Many individuals feel scared when requested to make their first public speech, yet these underlying feelings of trepidation can be reduced by their deftness which will also lay the foundation for making a powerful presentation.

A presentation is a method for communication that can be attuned to different situations, say, conversing with a gathering, tending to a meeting or briefing a group. A presentation can likewise be utilised as an expansive term that incorporates other 'talking engagements', like, making a speech at a wedding, or getting a point crosswise over in a video conference. To be effective, well-ordered preparation and the technique and method for introducing the data ought to be meticulously considered.

Preparing for the presentation is the most important highlight of the effective presentation. This incorporates the goal, the subject, the place, time and the Audience. You have been requested that give a presentation to a gathering of individuals. To begin with, ask yourself "why?" What is the reason for the presentation, what is the goal, what results do you and the gatherings of people anticipate? It is valuable to record the reason you have been requested in this meeting so you can utilise this for a steady update while you set up the presentation. There are many purposes behind giving a presentation or talk, yet never dismiss your goal as decided when you were asked and acknowledged the welcome. The goal is different from the subject.

Focus on the subject or the topic line which you need to present. The subject might be given to you by an enticing organisation. The subject might be altogether your decision inside specific restrictions. Before getting ready the material for a presentation, it merits considering your group of Audience.

Fitting your presentation to the group of Audience is vital and the accompanying focuses ought to be considered: The Size of the gathering or group of the Audience needs to be anticipated. The age run - a talk meant for senior citizen may not gel well with youth. Gender graduation, what will the gathering of people, will it be overwhelmingly male or female? Is it a captive group of Audience or they participate out of interest? Will you be talking into their workspace or recreation time? These are vital questions that have to be considered before giving a presentation

The Place: It is essential to have much prior information as could be expected about the venue where you will deliver the presentation. In a perfect world, attempt to mastermind to see the venue before the presentation, as it can be of incredible advantage of being acquainted with the environment. It does much to control fear in the event that you can envision the place while you are setting up your presentation. Furthermore, it would likewise give you the chance to experiment with your voice. On the off chance that at all conceivable, you have to know: The extent of the room. The seating arrangement and can suggest if they can be adjusted. The accessibility to all gadgets, speakers, laptop placement, overhead projector, Board Chart etc.

The accessibility of power points and an extension lead is required for any hardware you expect to utilise. In the event that the room has draperies or blinds. This is important that you plan to utilise visual guides, thus that you can guarantee the right mood for your presentation. Time and length of the presentation is of crucial importance to make a lasting impact on the Audience.

The morning is the best time to present since individuals are for the most part is generally ready. Be that as it may, a late morning presentation might be slightly tricky, as people feel hungry and consider lunch. The afternoon is not a perfect time to make presentations since after lunch individuals frequently feel sluggish and torpid. Mid-evening is a decent time, though toward the finish of the evening individuals may begin to stress over returning home, the activity or gathering youngsters from school.

Outside customary available time, individuals will probably be available in light of the fact that they need to be instead of must be there. There is a higher probability of gathering of people in the evening, given obviously that the presentation does not continue for a really long time when individuals may need to leave before the presentation is completed.

Before you compose your presentation, you have to arrange the structure by developing your thoughts and selecting the principle focus. You ought to employ your presentation with the primary message, the introduction, the content, and a conclusion. You need to include a story that has a most extreme effect and one which passes on your message in a way that is effectively comprehended by the target audience.

In public speaking and rhetorical debates, and additionally in much communication, the centre should have three principle components: Within the primary body of the presentation, partition key message into three components and after that expand each of these focuses into three sub-points. On the off chance that you are utilising a visual aid, for example, PowerPoint, limit the quantity of visual cues to three on every slide and develop each of these.

There is much to consider in choosing a proper presentation method. This incorporates utilising sound frameworks, like, how to oversee visual guides, how you stand, and how much communication you need with your audience. In settling on a choice about your presentation technique, you need to consider a few key aspects. a) The offices accessible to you by a method for visual guides, sound frameworks, and lights b) The event c) The group of audience, as far as both size and familiarity with you d)Your recognition with the subject.

There are some types in preparing for a presentation. These are essential in choosing these methods; Very formal presentation is one which is done at large conferences where the target audience is more than 300.Then there is the formal presentation which targets smaller conferences or groups where you don't know the audience. There is the Informal presentation, where it is a small group, probably internal, but not all known. The last is very informal presentation, where again the target audience is very small in size but the audience is familiar.

Whatever strategy you pick is generally directed by the event and its convention: A Very formal has a tendency to run with a larger audience, whose individuals you don't know well. Your part is probably going to be considerably more by giving data, and substantially less about having a discussion about the data.

It won't be conceivable, for example, to present to 200 individuals from a seat as a major aspect of the presentation, on the grounds that the vast majority of the group of the audience won't see or hear you. You have to apply judgment skills to your decision and the presentation strategy.

Presentation Notes: Whether you're sufficiently sure to talk with extremely short notes, or you require a full content, you have to consider how you record it to remind you what you will state. There are different cases of ways you may deal with your content a) Full-Text Notes b)Notes on Cue Cards c)Catchphrases on Cue Cards d) Mind Maps.

Many greatly skilled and sure presenters will let you know that they truly fear the question and answer session of a presentation. They look for approaches to "evade" troublesome inquiries. In any case, it doesn't need to be that way. Managing inquiries in a presentation is an ability which anybody can master. Maybe an essential thing to comprehend is that when in doubt if individuals make inquiries, even antagonistic ones, it's not to excursion you up but rather in light of the fact that they really need the reply.

Lectures offer a decent approach to give a lot of data to a major gathering in a short span of time. A seminar empowers group discussion and checking with the participants have they comprehended the subject in a much smaller gathering. Presentations have a tendency to be twenty to thirty minutes, trailed by a question session. Whereas lectures are relied upon to last the full span of the session, with zero assigned question time. The term of the session will be set by the institution maybe a couple hours.

A presentation has to capture the minds of the audience. The proven way is a presenter being mindful. A mindful presenter comprehends that it's insufficient to just talk at a group of people and show them slides. They create their presentation to connect with whatever number of our human faculties as could be allowed; particularly our feeling of sight given that impressive research proposes a large portion of us is visual learners.

This implies with regards to making slides they have a similar outlook as a fashion designer and make slides which are convincing, staggering and are certain to have an effect and be significant. They utilise short capable recordings which might be significant and enhance their target and goal. They utilise props, where pertinent and fitting, as they realise that getting their gathering of people to touch something of significance can have an enduring effect. They include them and make them feel part of the presentation by making inquiries, motivating them to think, envision and to investigate.

To conclude, the presentation strategies should cater to all of the learning styles since any audience will be of various combinations of the different types of learners.

Counseling

In General, youth are unenthusiastic to heed to any advice. But most of them are fond of giving advice. Many individuals will, at some moment in their lives, will try to prudently play a part of a Counsellor without having a genuine comprehension of the idea of what expert counselling necessitates.

There is a major distinction between an expert counsellor and a person who utilises some counselling skills of their part on a friend or a colleague. An expert counsellor is a prepared person who can utilise an alternate scope of advising methodologies with their clients. Let us examine which is counselling and which is not counselling. Counselling can thus be defined as the procedure that happens when a client and counsellor set aside time keeping in mind the end goal to dissect the troubles which may include the stress and/or Emotional sentiments of the client. The demonstration of helping the client to view things all the more distinctly from an alternate viewpoint. This can empower the customer to focus on emotions and behaviour, with an objective to encourage a positive change. A relationship of trust, keeping up privacy is imperative to productive counselling.

Proficient counsellors will generally clarify their approach to the time alone with the client, they may, in any case, be required by law to reveal data that they trust is risky to life of the client. Counsellor creates knowledge and comprehension in connection to self and environment, open to enhancing in regard to his possibilities and objectives he has picked.

Which is not Counselling?

Giving advice.

Being Judgmental.

Endeavouring to deal with the issues of the client.

Expecting or urging a client to carry on in a path in which the counsellor may have carried on when faced a similar issue in their own life.

Getting emotionally bonded with the client.

Dealing client issues from your own particular viewpoint, in light of the value system that the counsellor may follow.

Counselling can be a confusing term - it often has different meanings for different people.

The part of the counsellor is to empower the client to

investigate numerous aspects of their life and emotions, by talking uncomplicatedly and openly. Talking in such a way it is seldom conceivable with family or companions, who are probably going to be candidly included and have conclusions and predispositions that might be negative to the accomplishment of the counselling. It is vital that the Counsellor is not candidly integrated with the client and does not turn out to be so in the middle of counselling sessions. The counsellor neither judges nor offers any advice. The counsellor gives the client a chance to express worrying emotions, say, indignation, abhorrence, blame and fear in an off the record disposition.

The counsellor may urge the client to analyse the element of their lives that they may have discovered upsetting or difficult to confront recently. There might be some examination through investigation of earlier youth encounters with a specific end goal to throw some light on why an individual responds or reacts in certain courses in given circumstances. This is frequently tracked by well-considering routes in which the client may change such behaviour.

Powerful counselling decreases confusion, permitting the client to settle on successful choices prompting to positive changes in their behaviour as well as performance. Powerful counselling is not guidance giving and is not following up for another person's sake. A definitive point of counselling is to allow the client to settle on their own decisions, achieve their own particular choices and to follow up on their own accord.

Counselling takes the length it needs to. It would extremely be troublesome to put a time restriction on the measure of care, thinking space and consideration that a client may require. The more unpredictable and extreme is the issues that a client is managing.
This process may eat away time. Transient or temporary counselling, that endures a time of weeks or months, might be adequate for clients more goals oriented.
Longer-term counselling, in any case, will focus on the improvement of the client mental prosperity and identity.
There are types of counselling 1) Directive Counselling 2) Non – Order Counselling 3) Eclectic Counselling.

E.G WILLIAMSON is the chief exponent in this viewpoint. Counsellor –centred: the counsellor directs the client to take steps in order to resolve his conflicts. It is based on assumption that the client cannot solve his own problems for lack of information.
How do psychotherapy and counselling differ?
Counselling
Counselling is a systematic process which gives individuals an opportunity to explore, well-being discover and clarify ways of living more resourcefully with a greater happiness. Counselling may be concerned with addressing and resolving specific problems, making decisions, coping with crisis, co-workers working through conflict, or improving relations-workers. Counselling can be practiced within any

of the therapeutic approaches like psychoanalytical, systemic counselling.

People distinguish problem and crisis and urge them to find a way to determine these issues. It is the best course of helpful treatment for any individual who as of now has a comprehension of prosperity, and who is likewise ready to determine problems. Counseling is a procedure that energises the change of behaviour.

Psychotherapy:

It helps people with mental issues that have developed over the span of a drawn out stretch of time. It will help you comprehend your sentiments, considerations and activities more clearly. Psychotherapy is a more drawn out term procedure of treatment that distinguishes intense subject matters and the foundation to issues and challenges.

Essentials for Counselling Skills

Communication skills are obviously of extreme significance to counselors: active listening, clarification, reflection and effective questioning skills. Listening skill, disclosing skill referred to here as skill. The level of competence also means skilled or unskilled in this area. However, competence in a skill is best viewed not as an either which counselors as possessing the good skill or poor skill. In all skills areas, counselors are likely to possess mixtures of strengths and deficiencies. For instance, in the skills area of listening, counselors may be good at understanding clients but poor at showing their understanding. Similarly, in just about all areas of their functioning clients will possess a mixture of poor and good skills. Another meaning of skill relates to the knowledge and sequence of choices entailed in implementing the skill. The essential elements of any skill are the ability to make and implement sequences of choices to achieve objectives.

In the event that the counsellor is great at listening in profoundly and precisely to the clients, they need to settle on and actualize viable decisions in their attitude ranges. The question of counselling, treatment and training should be down to earth position work and necessary supervision is to help clients in the abilities zone and to stay more focused on the training to move more toward settling on great step forward instead of poor decisions. In the expertise region of dynamic counselling, the target is to empower customers to use sound judgment all the while, of implicit clients as well as in demonstrating the understanding to them.

Communication and action skill differ by the territory of utilisation, for example, listening abilities, summarising aptitudes, testing skills. There are a few approaches to which counselor and client can send communication and activity skill messages.

According to The UK Council for Psychotherapy, UKCP "Counselling and psychotherapy have helped many people deal with mental health issues or emotional distress, which can be experienced in many ways including:
• Anxiety or an inability to cope or concentrate
• Inability to deal with stress or recover from stressful

situations
- Lack of confidence or excessive shyness
- Coping with the effects of abuse
- Feelings of depression, sadness, grief or emptiness
- Extreme mood swings
- Difficulty making or sustaining relationships, or repeatedly becoming involved in unsatisfying or destructive relationships
- Difficulties in coming to terms with losses such as bereavement, divorce or loss of employment
- Eating disorders
- Self-harm

.Marital dispute
- Obsessive behavior
- Panic attacks and phobia
- Addiction"

These disorders are approached through various methods of counseling
- Psychodynamic counseling
- Humanistic counseling
- Client-centered counseling
- Cognitive-behavioural Counseling

Career Counseling for Students to choose their fitting skills.

Relationship counseling for strained marital relationship.

I have a personal experience in counseling many however dealing with quite a few who had the symptoms of PTSD because of December floods in Chennai was in fact demanding, as an NLP I inquired them to be open and express their misery. The challenge was to identify risk factors for developing prolonged stress disorders and in particular post-traumatic stress disorders.

Despite the fact that interests in self-advancement and empowerment are relentlessly developing there are still, sadly, many individuals who have assumptions about what counseling can offer and what is about, also, what it may or may not be able to. These myths and misinterpretations can frequently be sufficient to stop somebody getting to Counseling as a chance to empower and self-change; on the grounds that these thoughts will impact the potential client in a negative way.

To be a successful counselor, you'll have the capacity to make individuals feel relaxed in your presence and in addition being able to build a trusting association with them. To set up this relationship, you should be sensitive, calm and non-judgmental.

****

Selling to different Gene's

In the current economic atmosphere, India seems to be meticulous, all set to embrace a cashless digital economy. Competition is widespread and potential customers are increasingly willing to research and shop around in order to gain value for their hard-earned cash. Exceptional sales skills are of vital importance in this difficult environment. A job of a salesman stands out as amongst the most difficult employments, requiring the capacity to oversee a group of individuals who are, for the most part, high achievers and also have demanding identities. Salespersons are hired by their company; while customers are the end clients of the company. The saleable products as well as the organisations, each one of these people profits because of sales promotional activity.

An Organisation can be profitable only if its revenue surpasses its costs.

Compelling Sales managers need to perceive and maintain a strategic distance from basic authority botches, organise to duck the domination of the passionate, and comprehend the authentic, causative, and esteem based spikes on their sales people. The sales representative is confronted with different impulses; Customer modernity, furious rivalry, commoditization, value fixation, Sales target cycles and prevailing worldwide changes in purchasing practices. To gain from these potential outcomes, a sales representative must have predominant presenting skills—abilities that capture client trust and distinguish them from their rivals.

Numerous Sales people, particularly those who are new to sales, often take it too personal when a prospect says "NO" and they neglect to persevere with their endeavours while others transform prospecting into nuisance not knowing how to connect with a prospect successfully. In either case, these individuals are neglecting to be positive or continue to persistently position themselves with prospects in this way limiting their sales opportunities much further.

Sales techniques are the strategies that sales experts use to make income.

Cold calling is the way toward reaching a client that you have never addressed in the past and for which you have been given no referrals.

The sales strategy of noteworthy inquiries is utilised to keep the client required in the sales presentation. The sales professional needs to ask the customer questions that require some kind of response with respect to the outlook instead of a "yes" or "no" answer. The goal of this sales technique is to get the customer to state "yes" until the deal is closed. An essential sale technique is a capability to conquer the protests that can bring about negative answers.

A sales technique necessitates listening to what the client is stating keeping in mind the end goal to comprehend the criticism. The complaint being expressed can frequently be the after effect of a much more profound issue.

Sometimes, the least difficult sales techniques are the best. A sales professional should have the capacity to distinguish the opportune time to request the sale to close.

There are the basic elements of sales management:

Plan of Action: A business can't be taken as a risk. Each sales representative or individual concerned need to see the future in a planned way to accomplish deals. What's more, he has to decide the right person to take it further. The plan of action must be followed on broad marketing research, and the certainties must be confirmed at each stage. The ongoing plan ought to likewise be assessed, subsequent to exploring the overall market, for a specific kind of product. Adaptability must be given by building up a pro's generation line, to take into account the vagaries. The plan of action ought to be liable to be periodically reviewed. The points of interest of the plan ought to be discussed, with all the departmental heads, concerned, and their subordinates, who bear responsibilities regarding fulfilling their parts of the plan.

Coordination: Coordination is inescapable and pervades each capacity of the administration procedure. Coordination additionally helps in the most extreme usage of human exertion by the practice of powerful administration, direction, inspiration, supervision and communication. The control framework likewise needs coordination. Co-ordination does not have any unique methods. In any case, there are sound standards, on which to create skills. It has a unique need to help the staff, to see the aggregate picture and organise their exercises, with whatever remains of the group. The business director needs to empower coordinate individual contact, inside the association, especially where it is a horizontal authority. Amiability, and not friction, ought to be the directing mantra. Furthermore, one needs to guarantee a free stream of data that is specific to the goals of the business. No individual issues, emerging from business operations are to be overlooked, yet unravelled through a free trade of thoughts. This is particularly valid on account of any sales force of any organisation.

Controlling: A salesman makes a beeline to routinely check and ensures the business action is moving on the right course or not. He associates, leads, and inspires the subordinates. He needs to figure out how to ensure that the activities acclimate to the plan and target of the organisation. The control highlight should be the true objective that one can remove a sign from the past, note the pitfalls and take remedial measures, so that comparable issues may not occur later on. The controller needs to ensure that targets, expenses schedule and sales plan are accomplished and followed. There must be techniques to pass on the ability to achieve the objective. Each sales representative has a goal, set for specific 'period. From the step by step and month to month sales reports, the control system is developed, that will prepare records whether a particular sales representative is working profitably or not.

Inspiring: Motivation is basically a human resource. This concept intends to bind together particular identities into an effective group. For this, information of psychology is required, as a method for understanding behaviour. This is particularly critical on account of the sales team. Only an inspired salesman can accomplish organisation's objectives.

Of the numerous Sales Skills required, negotiation is especially important. Everyone employs negotiation occasionally; at work, at home, as a leader, as a salesman, and as a consumer. For some it appears to be simple, however, others see the procedure of transaction as a wellspring of contention to be opposed and kept away from if conceivable. The Negotiation is a procedure and an expertise that can be produced.

The negotiation can be portrayed as a procedure that includes at least two individuals managing each other with the goal of framing an understanding and a guarantee to a strategy where a compromise should become to further. In a sales domain, not each sales circumstance needs negotiation however when an understanding need to be achieved negotiation regularly includes a progression of communication between two parties to share an understanding of the points of interest of a sales solution. Selling to various Generations.

Baby Boomer, Gen X, Y, Z customers.

Blogger Nattie water worth states "The Baby Boomers are a period of people considered post-WWII 'Time of expanded birth rates', by and large amidst the years 1946 to 1964. In the years taking after WWII various western nations experienced a spike in births as they step by step recovered from the money related hardships experienced in the midst of wartime.

GEN X came after the Baby Boomers, and normally covers individuals conceived between the mid-1960 and the mid-1980s. Gen X was moulded by worldwide political occasions that happened amid this current era's childhood. This GEN recalls how TV murdered the radio and is more negative about having enough cash to retire. Gen Xers are occupied! They're managing kids, paying home loans and education loan for their off springs.

GEN Y came after Generation X. GEN-Y covers individuals conceived between the 1980's and the year 2000, and these people are some of the time alluded to as Gen Y, the Millennial Generation, or basically Millennial. GEN Y has been moulded by the innovative upheaval that happened all through their childhood. Gen Y grew up with innovation, so being associated and technically knowledgeable in their DNA. The millennia or the Gen Y customers are influenced by their peers. They seek peer input to influence decisions. Millennial are reshaping the way that products and services are being marketed by remaining inert to customary advertising strategies. This Generation chooses where to eat based on Instagram pictures, picks hairdressers from Face book and have their groceries delivered to their doorsteps in view of a suggestion from a peer.

GEN Z is the era of youngsters conceived after the Year 2000. They are the offspring of Generation X and Generation Y. To be reasonable we don't have the foggiest about the character attributes of Generation Z, since they haven't been on the earth for long yet. GEN Z are anticipated to be exceptionally associated, living during a time of cutting edge communication, innovation-driven ways of life and productive utilisation of online networking especially social media".

According to the study conducted by Capgemini on this "55.7% of Gen Y clients from Asia-Pacific are not certain they will stay with their essential bank in the following six months. Considering 30% of the worldwide populace, Generation Y is relied upon to be a noteworthy Earning power throughout the next decade. Gen Y uses innovation to meet their potential for all products and services, as a rule, banks are attempting to comprehend the business and innovation needs for this group".

It is essential to remember that every Generation contains remarkable identities, not all individuals will react a similar way. Try not to toss your other strategies and segmentation out the window! Ideally, these marketing tips will capture your target Generation. Salesmanship serves the dual purpose of discovering and persuading potential buyers. By his creative ability, a salesman has not only to sell but also establish a winning, regular and permanent relationship with his customers.

****

Public Speaking

Daniel Webster, an American Senator in the mid-nineteenth century, said "if every one of my abilities and forces were to be taken from me by some mysterious fate and if I am left with my decision of keeping, however, one, I would unhesitatingly make a request to be permitted to keep the power of public speaking, as it would rapidly recover the rest". Such is the supremacy of public Speaking. There are a lot of circumstances where great public speaking abilities can help you to propel your profession and make opportunities. Opportunities may range from, speaking about your organisation at a gathering, make a discourse subsequent to accepting an honor, or teaching a class to newcomers. Addressing a crowd of people additionally incorporates online introductions or talks; for example, when training a virtual group, or when addressing a gathering of clients in a web-based meeting.

Great public speaking skills are essential in different aspects of your life. But a large number of individuals have a strong fear to articulate. The capacity to stand up before a crowd and successfully impart your thoughts is one of the outright rawest types of force that influences people and hold you in good stead.

At first, we can look into the two key objectives of public speaking. Outlining clear introductions, conveying them in an engaging way. You can think about these as the essential. Presently, more particularly, we have the target. Along these lines, the primary target is, you ought to have the capacity to outline and convey fundamental presentation plainly.

The vast majority of us don't ponder giving impromptu speeches until we've been put on the spot and by then, it's past the point of no return. Consider a portion of the conceivable situations when you might be called upon, surprisingly, to offer a couple comments or to give an impromptu: an impromptu is sudden and in light of the fact that it will probably just last a couple of minutes. Many psychologists propose the fear of Public Speaking follows back to primal instincts from the cave-dwelling human race. A public-speaking situation basically puts the speaker separated from a gathering, bearing all the consideration of a group of people.

We learned sometimes impromptu speeches can be dubious. Finding the correct words without notification ahead of time may not be that easy for each speaker. No worry. The <u>Extemporaneous speech</u> is a perfect balance this is a flawless pitch. This speech includes the speaker's utilization of notes and some adornment to convey a point. To clear this up, a speaker who utilizes this strategy would have note cards or prompts that guide him from indicating a point, yet he utilizes his own words as he goes along.

Commemorative Speech

Commemorative Speeches are now and then known as "Ceremonial" or "epideictic" addresses. And no more essential level, commemorative pay tribute or acclaim a man, an establishment, an occasion, thought, or place. Their attention is on "VALUES". All social orders hold certain qualities integral to human presence: magnificence, dependability, astuteness, generosity, convention, achievement, honesty, experience, and fearlessness, for instance. The memorial speeches will commend these qualities. Sorts of memorial talks incorporate the commendation, the speeches of designation, the speeches of goodwill, the wedding, and the honor acknowledgment speeches and few more.

Informative Speeches

Informative speeches describe, define, analyze, tell how to use, and synthesize. Imagining sitting in the gathering of people tuning into your teacher discussing the hypothesis of refraction of light. It might seem like confounding words to many; however, what he is truly doing is giving an informative speech. This sort of speech is given to the gathering of people about something they don't definitely know. Speeches may address a) Addresses about objects b) Addresses about occasions c) Addresses about procedures d) Addresses about concepts. At the point when a public speaker can motivate your faculties, similar to touch, smell or feel, it is an address about objects and includes discussing things about the sensory and physical world. If a speaker describes the IPL match he witnessed the previous day he is addressing about an event. If you happen to watch a cooking program on TV you would surely understand this is the process. Some are speeches are about concepts, written about theoretical ideas and notions, like world peace, freedom or love. Unlike the other types of informative speeches, this type of speech is intangible.

Demonstrative Speeches – This has numerous similitudes with informative speeches. A demonstrative speech likewise teaches something. The principle contrast lies in including a showing of how to do the thing you're teaching or training. A few cases of demonstrative speeches: The most effective method to begin your page in a social media. The most efficient method to prepare a pudding.

Persuasive Speeches

Persuasive speech is a particular kind of talk in which the speaker has an objective of persuading the group of onlookers to acknowledge his or her perspective. The speech is masterminded so as to ideally bring about the audience to acknowledge the idea. Despite the fact that the general objective of a persuasive speech is to persuade the audience to acknowledge a point of view, not all people can be persuaded by a solitary speaking session and not all viewpoints can convince the crowd. The achievement of a persuasive speech is frequently measured by the gathering of people's readiness to consider the speaker's contention. Rhetorical Appeals, Ethos, Pathos, and Logos are modes of persuasion used to convince audiences.

Ethos or the moral interest intends to persuade an audience of the creator's validity or character. A creator would utilize ethos to show to his gathering of people that he is a trustworthy source and merits tuning in to. Ethos can be created by picking dialect that is proper for the audience and theme making you sound reasonable or fair-minded.

Pathos intends to convince a crowd of people by speaking to their feelings. Creators utilize pathos to conjure sensitivity from the audience; to make the group of onlookers feel what the creator needs them to feel. A typical utilization of feeling is drawn feel sorry for from a crowd of people. Another utilization of feeling is motivated outrage from a crowd of people; maybe with a specific end goal to provoke activity.

Logos or the interest to the rationale intends to persuade a crowd of people by utilization of logic or reasoning. To utilize logos is refer to truths and measurements, verifiable and strict analogies, and referring to specific experts on a subject we should see a couple of illustrations here to understand these styles.

Our PM Shri Narendra Modi utilized Ethos to announce Demonetisation, referring to it as the mechanism that will bring out Black Money, fake money and it would not help terrorist activities. Seeing the dependability of the person and the proclamation, people wilfully cooperated for over 2 months. Recently we were all enthralled by the great achievement of ISRO scientist for successfully launched more than 100 satellites in a rocket; our leaders emotionally (Pathos) paid rich honours on this achievement. "You ought to consider another course. I heard that that road is significantly more risky and inauspicious during the evening than amid the daytime". There is no room for any complacency; in my experience of over 2 decades, we need to visit the construction site to understand the problem better. This example relates to logos.

An effective speaker will do their best to set up solid ethos with their audience, and combine pathos and logos to shape an ideal contention. Assessing the audience is a vital parameter when giving a persuasive speech. Odds are that you'll once in a while need to talk out in the open as a feature of your role.

While this can appear to be scaring, the advantages of having the capacity to talk well exceed any apparent feelings of fear. To improve as a speaker, utilize the accompanying methodologies:

Planning, Hone, Draw in with your Audience, Focus on non-verbal communication. Think emphatically, Adapt to your nerves. Watch recordings of your speeches. In the event that you talk well out in the open, it can help you land a position or advancement, bring issues to light for your group or association, and teach others. The more you drive yourself to talk in front of others, the better you'll get to be, and the more certainty you'll have. Entertainment Speeches: The speaker gives joy and delight that make the gathering of people giggle or relate to episodic data. Mimicry being the best model for entertainment.

The <u>Policy speech</u> is a type of persuasive speech with a couple of specific differences. In the first place, in the Policy Speech, you should advocate a change in government strategy while in the Persuasive Speech you can advocate for all intents and purposes anything: an adjustment in the arrangement, an adjustment in your audience's convictions, a change in audience activities, and so forth. Second, in the Policy Speech, you should react to contentions against your speech while in the Persuasive Speech you react to inquiries regarding your persuasion. Third, in the Policy Speech, you have to utilize certain sorts of contentions and considerably more data and documentation than in the Persuasive Speeches.

In <u>a manuscript speech</u>, the speaker peruses each word from a pre-written speech. This appears to be sufficiently simple. All things considered, if your audience appreciates, it might work. Perusing straightforwardly from the pages of a script has its advantages. You won't miss a solitary word or essential truth. The drawback? It can be exhausting and soporific. Without eye contact, activity or development in front of an audience may get to be distinctly unengaged. This is particularly valid if the speech is a drab boring subject.

Speaking in public is a learnable skill. Learning the above types of speeches in detail, you can become a better speaker and presenter.

****

Anticipating Risk

Risk management is the method of appraisal, and prioritization of risks pursued by the management. It can be defined as the composed and prudent use of a cost-effective application is to minimise, screen, and control the likelihood of unforeseen events or to augment the recognition of an opportunity. In other words, Risk Management is to ponder what could turn out badly, and deciding how likely as well as disastrous that would be and making a calculated move to stay away from either the issue or its outcomes. Risk management is to guarantee stability, and it does not deviate from the main business goals.

Refer to this instance for better comprehension; a decision by the management requires a new technology be developed. The calendar shows 8 months for this action, however, the specialised workers confide that 12 months is nearer to reality. In the event that the project head is proactive, the group will build up an alternate course of action right at this point. They will create answers for the issue of time before the project due date. In spite of the fact, the project administrator is receptive, and then the group will do nothing until the issue really happens. The project will approach its 8 months deadline; many works will even now be uncompleted, even if the project chief responds quickly to this emergency, bringing about the group to lose significant time.

"Risk comes from not knowing what you're doing" -Warren Buffet. He alludes that risk is a by-product of ignorance. Furthermore, there is a straightforward answer for that i.e.; a truly extensive risk analysis and further laying a solid strategy for dealing with those dangers. This is really a genuinely straightforward process.

The basic point is that Risk Management is a persistent procedure and it should not only be done at the beginning of the project, yet should be periodically done for the entire duration of the project. For instance, if a project aggregates a span evaluated at 6 months, a risk appraisal ought to be done in any event toward the finish of every month. At every phase of the project life, the new risk will be recognised, evaluated and managed. An ideal approach to do a Risk Management is with each one of those involved in the project. Just that way it would be able to have a sensible and complete discussion with every one of the risks and how to alleviate them.

The reason for risk management is to:
a) Distinguish conceivable risks.

b) Reduce or allocate risk.

c) Give a sound premise to better basic leadership for all threats.

Planning for exigencies

Assessing and managing risks are the best weapons you have against project debacle. By evaluating your projection for potential issues and creating techniques to address them, you'll enhance your odds of a fruitful, if not flawless, extend.

Risk Response, for the most part, incorporates: *Avoidance*; disposing of a particular danger, generally by dispensing with the cause. *Mitigating*: lessening the normal money related estimation of a risk by decreasing the likelihood of an event. *Acknowledgement*: tolerating the outcomes of the Risk. This is regularly built up by a professional in the emergency, the course of action to execute when the Risk situation happens.

The most effective method is to do Risk Management

To begin with, we have to take into consideration the various roots of Risks. There are many sources and this rundown is not intended to be comprehensive, but instead, is a guide to understand the underlying concepts behind risks. By referencing this rundown, it helps the group to decide every conceivable source of risk.

There are various sources in which risk may arise, let see some of them here; External Risks, these are unpredictable, unanticipated administrative prerequisites, Natural calamity, Vandalism, undermine or unpredicted reactions are considered risks which anyone is not prepared. Predictable threats happen from marketing or Risk in Operation, some arising out of Social references, Ecological variances, Cost escalation, Currency fluctuation, Press and Social media.

Technical Threats is another area in which you can anticipate risk; Examples include Innovative changes happening in departments, there may be threats originating from the process, Legal hitch, infringement of Trade Mark, legal issues on breach of contract and labour or work environment issue. Apart from these threats, there are threats which arise out of the project. The top managing administration not perceiving this activity as a project. An excessive number of undertakings going ahead at one time. Incomprehensible timetable responsibilities. No useful contribution to planning and implementation. No individual is assigned responsibility for the total project. Poor control of process configuration changes. Issues with colleagues. Poor control of client changes. Poor understanding of the project head. Wrong individual allocated as project chief. The above shows a glimpse of the risks that one can face

The Risk Analysis Process is basically a quality critical thinking, problem-solving process. Quality and evaluation tools are utilised to decide and organise risks for appraisal and resolution

a) Identifying the Risk

b) Assessing the Risk

c) Developing Responses to the Risk

d) Developing a Contingency Plan or Preventative Measures for the Risk.

Identifying the risk: This step is conceptualising. Evaluating the list of conceivable risk sources and additionally based on the project teams experience and understanding, every single potential risk is recognised. Utilising assessment tools, risks are then arranged and organised. The quantities of the risks distinguished are more often than the time limit of the project, here the project team has to split the priorities and provide contingencies. The procedure of prioritisation helps them to deal with those risks that have both a high effect and a high likelihood of the risk happening.

Assessing the risk, here is the conventional problem solving, it frequently moves from problem recognisable to problem solution, before attempting to decide how best to oversee risks, the project group must recognise the underlying drivers of the distinguished risks. What might trigger the risk? In what issue will the identified risk affect the project. Presently the project managing team is prepared to start the way toward assessing the conceivable solutions and the ways in which the risk or potentially happening, keep the various risks in mind. There may be certain queries like what should be possible to decrease the probability of this risk? What should be possible to deal with the risk, would it happen? These are considered as developing responses to the risk.

Build up a Contingency Plan or Preventative Measures for the Risk. The project management group will convert those thoughts that are recognised to diminish or dispose of risk possibilities into easy tasks. Those tasks recognised to deal with the risk if it happens, are created into short alternate courses of action that can be set aside. If the anticipated risk happens they can be presented and rapidly put off without hesitation, along these lines reducing the need to deal with the risk in case of any emergency.

As a major aspect of dealing with the health and security of any business, you should control the risks in your working environment. To do this you have to consider what may hurt individuals and choose whether you are finding a way to keep that damage. This is known as sensible evaluation of risks and it is something you are required by law to do. In the event that you have less than five workers, you don't need to record everything.

A risk management is not about making mountains of printed material, yet rather about recognising sensible measures to control the threats in your work environment. You are presumably effectively finding a way to ensure your workers; however, your risk appraisal will help you to choose whether you have secured all you have to.

Consider how an accident and sickness could happen and focus on genuine risks and those that are in all probability which will bring about the most disturbance. The Risk management is the reasoning about 'what could turn out badly, and what should we do to avert it?' ought to be a key a portion of any strategy advancement. It should be vital to your association at all levels.

Risk management standards have been created by a few associations, including the National Institute of Standards and Technology and the ISO. These models are intended to help associations recognize the particular threat, assess the kind of vulnerabilities to decide their risk, distinguish approaches to lessen these dangers and after that execute risk diminishment endeavours as indicated by the authoritative system. It's awful having the best risk management on the planet if no one has perused it, and no one makes a move.

****

Conclusion

As I fulfil this book comprising of brief essays on Soft Skills, this was targeted just to benefit individuals of different backgrounds. In today's situation Stress Management, Emotional Intelligence, Communication capability is the important requirement for general public. The proceeds of this book will go in encouraging me in bringing innovative intervention to soft skill training methodology and recording it. I hereby request your open-minded support for this book. Thank you to such an extent.

****

Made in the USA
Middletown, DE
31 July 2017